Studies in Educational Theory of the John Dewey Society

NUMBER 7

Ralph Barton Perry on Education for Democracy

*The Commission on Studies in Educational Theory
Appointed by the John Dewey Society*

Frederick Ellis
Western Washington State College

Ward Madden
*Brooklyn College,
The City University of New York*

Israel Scheffler
Harvard University

Robert Mason, Chairman
University of Pittsburgh

Ralph Barton Perry on Education for Democracy

by IRA S. STEINBERG

OHIO STATE UNIVERSITY PRESS

Standard Book Number: 8142-0014-1
Library of Congress Catalogue Card Number: 70-79847
Printed in the United States of America
Copyright © 1970 by the Ohio State University Press
All Rights Reserved

Thank you, Priscilla

Foreword

The heroes of the mind are too little known to the public. The quiet scholar in particular tends, in every age, to be overshadowed by statesman and soldier, story-teller and preacher, artist and magician. To this tendency we have, in our own time, added a special, and ironic, momentum: our expansion of education has accelerated specialization, our advancement of research has nourished a technological rather than a philosophical frame of mind. We have not, it seems to me, sufficiently nurtured an appreciation of our broad intellectual and scholarly traditions nor adequately cultivated the respect for general ideas.

Nor will appeal to the urgency of current crises justify this condition. On the contrary, to cope with challenge requires inner strength as well as outward alertness, self-awareness as well as the efficient handling of instrumentalities. It calls not only for a grasp of the immediate problem, but for a philosophical, historical, and moral perspective within which the problem can be located and assessed. The more critical our situation, the more urgent is the educational need to make available the thought of our scholars who have struggled to achieve such a perspective.

This is the need to which the present work of Dr. Steinberg is addressed. It offers an interpretation of an important American philosopher who, in responding to the issues and predicaments of the modern world, yet strove for the largest perspective on human life, a viewpoint at once scientific and moral, historical and contemporary, rational and humane, by which our specific problems might be illuminated and our choices made clear.

Ralph Barton Perry's thought was both deep and broad, ranging from a consideration of subtle issues in epistemology and value theory to a concern with the moral and practical problems of society. He contributed important theoretical analyses of the foundations of democracy and stimulating interpretations of intellectual history. In all that he wrote, he combined an astringent realism and respect for fact with a comprehensive sensitivity to the claims of human values. The present volume provides a full-scale examination of Perry's philosophy, from the vantage point of a dominant interest in its educational import.

Dr. Steinberg places Perry's educational ideas in the framework of his general philosophy, interpreting his epistemological, moral, and social views as a background for consideration of his educational opinions. The special focus on democracy is faithful to Perry's concerns, in which the democratic ideal occupies a central place.

Dr. Steinberg's work is critical and not merely expository. He gives a scholarly account of the views he discusses, but goes beyond mere description to interpretation and evaluation. If his own critical opinions cannot, in the nature of the case, be expected to elicit universal agreement, they can surely be expected to evoke serious reflection on issues fundamental to a free society. And in interpreting Perry's work to a wider public of educators, Dr. Steinberg offers a persuasive stimulus to the search for philosophical perspective and, thus, to the enhancement of our own educational thought and practice.

Israel Scheffler

Harvard University

Acknowledgments

I would like to express my appreciation to those whose assistance facilitated the preparation of this manuscript. It was presented in an earlier version as a doctoral dissertation to the faculty of the Graduate School of Education of Harvard University. Fellow students, friends, and faculty provided a forum through which ideas and positions could be sorted out and clarified. Mrs. Vada Rogers typed the original manuscript. The current version was developed during my stay as a Fellow of the Center for Advanced Study in the Behavioral Sciences at Stanford, California, and I thank the trustees of the Center for providing the necessary clerical and secretarial assistance. I thank also the members of the Commission on Studies in Educational Theory of the John Dewey Society for their suggestions and comments on the revision of the original manuscript.

I am particularly indebted to Ralph Barton Perry and Israel Scheffler. The former provided an opportunity to deal in depth with a set of positions with which I was, and in large measure still am, basically sympathetic. Professor Scheffler's advice and criticism have, hopefully, made my efforts less imprecise and ineffectual than they might have been otherwise. Although I never met Perry, I should like to think that these two men have taught me whatever I know about what it means to be a philosopher.

I gratefully acknowledge permission to quote from the following works by Ralph Barton Perry:

General Theory of Value. Quotations from this work have been reproduced with the permission of Harvard University Press, who reissued the title in 1950.

"A Note on Neutralism." From STRUCTURE, METHOD AND MEANING: Essays in Honor of Henry M. Sheffer, edited by Paul Henle, Horace M. Kallen, Suzanne K. Langer, copyright, 1951, by the Liberal Arts Press, Inc., reprinted by permission of The Bobbs-Merrill Company, Inc.

Present Philosophical Tendencies: A Critical Survey of Naturalism, Idealism, Pragmatism, and Realism with a Synopsis of the Philosophy of William James. Quotations from this work have been reproduced with the permission of Mr. Bernard B. Perry. A reprint edition was published by Greenwood Press, New York, in 1968.

Puritanism and Democracy. Reprinted by permission of the publisher, The Vanguard Press, from "Puritanism and Democracy" by Ralph Barton Perry. Copyright, 1944, by Ralph Barton Perry.

"Realism in Retrospect," *Contemporary American Philosophy: Personal Statements.* Quotations from this work have been reproduced with the permission of Russell & Russell, Publishers, who issued a reprint of this title in 1962.

Realms of Value: A Critique of Human Civilization. Reprinted by permission of the publishers from Ralph

Barton Perry, *Realms of Value: A Critique of Human Civilization*, Cambridge, Mass.: Harvard University Press, Copyright, 1954, by the President and Fellows of of Harvard College.

Table of Contents

Note to the Reader

The manuscript that follows is primarily philosophical and theoretical in style and content. The exposition of Perry's philosophical views and his views on education is intertwined with the critique of these views. In order to approach anything like an adequate philosophical understanding and critique of Perry's educational theory as education for democracy, it is necessary first to come to grips with his realism, his theory of value and his theory of society. Still, the reader with a more immediate or practical interest in theory of education might wish to begin by skimming through Chapters V and VI in order to gain an overview of the relevance of Perry's philosophy to the current educational scene before tackling the manuscript from the beginning.

Perry was quite prolific in the quantity of his publications. Still, the various aspects of his philosophy appeared in their clearest and most systematically organized forms in three major works. As it is the intention here to deal with Perry's most considered views and positions, rather than to detail their evolution, these works have been taken as the chief sources of material for discussion. It is worth noting that Perry himself indicated repeatedly in footnotes the great extent to which the positions advanced in earlier publications were incorporated, enlarged upon, and/or revised in these major works. These are cited here in full and abbreviated as follows:

GTV *General Theory of Value: Its Meaning and Basic Principles Construed in Terms of Interest* (New York: Longmans, Green, and Co., 1926).

PD *Puritanism and Democracy* (New York: The Vanguard Press, 1944).

RV *Realms of Value: A Critique of Human Civilization* (Cambridge: Harvard University Press, 1954).

I. Ralph Barton Perry: An Introduction

Ralph Barton Perry had a long and varied career. Educators are likely to remember him as a champion of liberal education. Philosophers will think of him primarily as the author of the classic "Ego-Centric Predicament" and as the most articulate and systematic proponent of interest theory in ethics. Members of the general academic community might remember him in many ways. He was the Pulitzer prize-winning biographer of William James. He was a super-patriot and propagandist for the American cause in two world wars. He was one of the first to protest the firing of faculty members who declined to testify before Congressional committees investigating subversive activities and was subsequently accused of having been a Communist himself. He was the chairman of the Universities Committee on Postwar International Problems.

Perry was an academic philosopher and a philosopher who wrote as well for the broad public. As an academic he was primarily a theorist. As a citizen he was an activist and an advocate. Yet it was hard for him to separate his theorizing from his advocacy. He believed in democracy. He did not, however, confine his belief merely, as many of us do, to a sort of mystical devotion to a set of liberal and humanistic ideals. He did not merely point to the historical development of popular democracy in the past few centuries as evidence for its claim upon the continuing and expanding allegiance of men in centuries to come. He went further and attempted to provide a systematic groundwork on which to base faith in democracy. He looked on education as both the means for promulgating that faith and as the means for equipping men to be the sorts of citizens who could and would justify that faith in act and deed.

Perry directed much of his effort as a philosopher and as an educator to the study and the promotion of particular aims and policies for education in a democracy. As suggested he took his ideals of democracy, humanism, morality and rationality quite seriously to heart. And, he did not compartmentalize them. Accordingly, if we are to appreciate his views on education, we must come to understand them in the context of his broad philosophical commitments. In particular we shall examine his theory of value, theory of society, and theory of education and their relationships. These theories represent a major portion, if not the major portion, of his works, and his interests in them were dominant themes throughout his career.

Before we turn directly to the exposition and analysis of these theories, we must first set the scene. Perry's own general philosophical orientation developed in reaction to two major philosophical positions at the turn of the century: idealism and pragmatism. He rejected idealism and, though brought up on pragmatism, he criticized it for its limitations. He sought to forge a new position, the New Realism, in opposition to idealism and as a corrective of pragmatism. Let us first try to understand why and also how he rejected idealism. Then in the next chapter we shall examine the more positive aspects of New Realism and the realistic critique of pragmatism.

From the vantage point of middle age Perry wrote:

> Such philosophical nourishment as I received in early youth was derived from Emerson and Carlyle. From them I caught no hint of transcendental metaphysics, but only a desire to be heroic. This influence, together with an intense adolescent religious experience, brought me to the threshold of manhood with a vague eagerness "to do good," or to contribute something to the triumph of that cause of righteousness which I identified with Christianity.[1]

His faith remained intact in what he termed his "pre-natal philosophical experience" at Princeton but with his migration to Harvard he entered upon a "perilous spiritual adventure, an abrupt transition from faith to criticism." [2] As is seen in the passage below his faith was altered rather than destroyed:

> Here for the first time, something happened to my *mind*, and the vocation of the ministry was gradually transformed, without reaction or bitterness, into that of the teacher and scholar. Creeds and dogmas having become impossible, I thought that I had found a way in which I might think freely and still "do good." It is that naive hope that has sustained me ever since.[3]

Leaving aside for the moment Perry's eagerness "to do good," what happened to Perry's mind? The faculty at Harvard during this period of Perry's life boasted such luminaries as James, Royce, Palmer, Santayana, Münsterberg and Everett. But, for most of the students the choice was between Royce and James. Perry chose the way of James. The impact of James, the teacher, upon Perry, his student, is beautifully illustrated as follows:

> To specify my indebtedness to James, is as impossible as it would be to enumerate the traits which I have inherited from my parents . . . I should like, however, to record the most vivid of the doctrinal impressions which he left upon me in the early days. I can remember even the stage-setting—the interior of the room in Sever Hall, the desk with which the lecturer took so many liberties, and the gestures with which James animatedly conveyed to us the intuition of *common-sense realism*. From that day I confess that I have never wavered in the belief that our perceptual experience disclosed a common world, inhabited by our perceiving bodies and our neighbors, and qualified by the evidence of our senses.[4]

This, then, was the direction Perry was to follow. In order to appreciate the full meaning of Perry's choice of direction it is necessary to pick up a thread previously left suspended—his desire "to do good"—and his aversion to the way of Royce. Perry was convinced that to follow Royce was to make the notion of doing good meaningless. He could not accept the position that 'all turns out for the best' as he read the idealism of his day. He insisted upon the obligation of men to bring their intelligence to bear to contrive practical means to eliminate evil and suffering and to make the world good.

For Perry, realism involved at least three things: the sense of purpose, the rejection of idealism, and the embracing of the role of science for philosophy. The position might be taken that the rejection of idealism was instrumental to and incidental to the desire to be scientific. On the surface this seems a reasonable contention. Certainly, if idealism stands in the way of being scientific, its rejection was crucial to those advocating the introduction "into philosophy of the two methods that had been so profitably employed in science: the method of co-operative work and the method of isolating problems and tackling them one by one." [5] Yet while the author of this quotation, Montague, could construe New Realism as involving strictly methodological criteria for the examination of epistemological theses,[6] Perry's sense of purpose led him further. He was concerned with the rejection of idealism not merely to permit his *confrères* and himself to pursue philosophy in a particular manner, but to overthrow idealism in order to harness, as it were, philosophical endeavor toward contributions to the good of mankind. He wished to destroy once and for all the hold of idealism on the minds of men.

Now this is not to say that Perry's rejection of idealism was not instrumental to his embracing of scientific method in philosophy. It is pointed out, however, that it was more than incidental to the latter aim. It is of significance to note that it was in the process of criticizing Royce's *The World and the Individual* [7] that Perry was credited with having fired "the first literary gun in the notable campaign of avowed realism against idealism. . . ." [8] Here in 1902 were set forth the basic themes and problems which were to occupy the New Realists for several years thereafter. Realism seems to have taken on shape in its rejection of idealism.

In the light of these considerations it would appear that a closer look at Perry's work *contra* idealism is appropriate both for gaining an appreciation of the merits of his argument, and as providing a context for the content of his realism. Perry's argument is epitomized in his article, "The Ego-Centric Predicament." [9] In his words, "This was a successful bit of phrase-making, if one is to judge by the frequency with which it has been misunderstood." [10] Yet, as will be seen, the analysis employed therein is ingeniously simple:

> *Ontological idealism* is best expressed by the proposition: Every thing (T) is defined by the complex, I know T. . . . In order to make it plain that the term [I] is generalized, . . . substitute ego, or E, for the pronoun. The term T is primarily distinguished from the other terms only in that it has unlimited denotation; it refers to anything and everything. It is desirable that the operation or relation "know" should be freed from its narrower intellectualist meaning; and it will, therefore, prove convenient to use the expression R^c, to mean any form of consciousness that relates to an object . . . Ontological idealism is . . . a name for the proposition $(E)R^c(T)$ defines T.[11]

Moreover it is this specific relation R^c and not some or all other possible relations of E to T which is essential in ontological idealism for defining T. Perry thus continued:

> Ontological idealism, then, is a theory to the effect that T necessarily stands in the relation R^c to an E, or that the relationship $R^c(E)$ is indispensable to T. Now the attempt to prove this theory at once reveals a predicament that might otherwise escape notice. One must attempt to discover the precise nature of the modification of T by $R^c(E)$; but one promptly encounters the fact that $R^c(E)$ can not be eliminated from one's field of study because "I study," "I eliminate," "I think," "I observe," "I investigate," etc. are all cases of $R^c(E)$. . . . Science has occasion to eliminate errors of judgment and relativities of sense, but has no occasion to eliminate

consciousness altogether; and therefore has not discovered that it is impossible.[12]

Perry concluded from this that rather than showing that there are no instances of things out of this relationship, it is more proper to recognize that one would "not be able to discover them if there were."[13] This is a methological predicament and not a solution to any problem. He brought this home sharply in the following:

> Just in so far as I do actually succeed in eliminating every cognitive relationship, I am unable to observe the result. Thus if I close my eyes I can not see what happens to the object; If I stop thinking I can not think what happens to it; and so with every mode of knowledge. In thus eliminating all knowledge I do not experimentally eliminate the thing known, but only the possibility of knowing whether that thing is eliminated or not.[14]

Perry went further in his analysis of the idealistic proposition and identified differing conceptions of idealism which he labelled as follows: "The *creative* theory asserts that E creates T; the *identity* theory asserts that E is T."[15] In each case he was able to reduce the arguments for these theories to the point where they become embroiled in the egocentric predicament and the attempt at escape through what he termed the fallacy of "definition by initial predication"—in this instance to assign the major or central role to knowing because in discourse it precedes the object known.[16]

The underlying arguments in idealism having been questioned in terms of a generalized ego, it is evident that the effort to evade the obvious subjectivism of the proposition through the mediation of an Infinite or Absolute mind represents little more than a refined mysticism. The term "anyone" can just as well refer to such an absolute. If it was not for such a notion as *"esse is percipi"* [17] there would be no need for the fabrication of an all-seeing mind to hold the world together in synthetic unity while mere mortals remain in ignorance of the universe in its entirety.

It is only a short step from the assumption of such an all-seeing mind to the assumption that what this mind sees is therefore good.[18] Who would dare question the goodness of that spirit which sees all and thereby causes all to exist? Question first, however, whether there is any proof for the contention that knowing in any of its forms is thereby constitutive of the object known, and this magnificent edifice crumbles. The existence of such a spirit is seen as wishful thinking to account for human inability to overcome the egocentric predicament. To defend such a spirit is to wallow in this predicament and not to resolve it. Further, it implies that such a predicament does not exist and in effect is prejudicial to efforts to extend human knowledge of the universe by branding such efforts as of no good purpose. (Unless, of course, it was admitted that such extensions of human knowledge might lift some of the burdens from the shoulders of our poor old universal spirit; but then too it might give him, or it, something else to think about.)

The claim might be made that there is a certain prejudice or bias in Perry's argument stemming from the simple fact that it was analysis. Thus it might be held that Perry, by subjecting the tenets of idealism to analysis, thereby denied, out of hand, the existence of the universal spirit.[19] Whether or not he wished to do so is not the issue here. His analysis merely showed that idealism was not entitled to the distinction of having proved its case. Insofar as its proponents presented arguments for idealism, their arguments were the proper subject for examination. Insofar as these arguments failed to support the idealist proposition, this proposition lacked proof. If this weakened the hold of idealism over the beliefs of man, it remained for the proponents of idealism to produce better arguments or to recognize that the proof of idealism lay beyond the capacity of man to construct.

The argument of the Ego-Centric predicament suggested the latter and ended on the following note:

> I have not undertaken to do more than to isolate a species of dangerous reasoning that infests a certain region of philosophical inquiry. The question of the precise modification which a thing undergoes when it is known, is a proper problem . . . but nothing whatsoever can be inferred . . . from the mere fact that nothing can be found that is thus not modified. . . . We cannot employ a method which in other cases proves a convenient preliminary step, the empirical, denotative method of agreement and difference. There remains, however, the method which must eventually be employed in any exact investigation, the method of analysis. . . . Having discovered just what an ego is, just what a thing is, and just what it means for an ego to have a thing, we may hope to define precisely what transpires when a thing is known by an ego. And until these more elementary matters have been disposed of we shall do well to postpone an epistemological problem that is not only highly complicated but of crucial importance for the whole system of philosophical knowledge.[20]

The rejection of idealism served to provide a justification for the activities undertaken by the New Realists. We turn next to an examination of these activities as they comprised the content of New Realism.

1. Ralph Barton Perry, "Realism in Retrospect," *Contemporary American Philosophy: Personal Statements*, ed. George P. Adams and William Pepperell Montague (2 vols.; New York: Macmillan Co., 1930), II, 187.

2. Ibid.

3. Ibid.; Perry's italics.

4. Ibid., p. 189.

5. William Pepperell Montague, "Confessions of an Animistic Materialist," *Contemporary American Philosophy*, II, 145.

6. Ibid.

7. Josiah Royce, *The World and the Individual* (New York: Macmillan Co., 1900–1901), and the critique, Ralph Barton Perry, "Professor Royce's Refutation of Realism and Pluralism," *Monist*, Vol XII, No. 3 (1902).

8. Victor E. Harlow, *A Bibliography and Genetic Study of American Realism* (Oklahoma City: Harlow Publishing Co., 1931), p. 20.

9. Ralph Barton Perry, "The Ego-Centric Predicament," *Journal of Philosophy, Psychology and Scientific Methods*, Vol. VIII, No. 1 (1910), and cf. the following: Wendell T. Bush, "The Problem of the Egocentric Predicament," *Journal of Philosophy, Psychology, and Scientific Methods*, Vol. VI, No. 16 (1911), Mary Whiton Calkins, "The Idealist to the Realist," *Journal of Philosophy, Psychology, and Scientific Methods*, Vol. VIII, No. 17 (1911), John Dewey, "The Short Cut to Realism Examined," *Journal of Philosophy, Psychology, and Scientific Methods*, Vol. VII, No. 20 (1910), and E. B. McGilvary, "Realism and the Egocentric Predicament," *Philosophical Review*, Vol. XXI, No. 3 (1912).

10. Perry, *Contemporary American Philosophy*, II, 192.

11. Perry, *Journal of Philosophy, Psychology, and Scientific Methods*, VIII, No. 1, 5–6.

12. Ibid., p. 7; Perry's quotes.

13. Ibid., p. 8; Perry's italics.

14. Ibid.

15. Ibid., pp. 9 ff.; Perry's italics.

16. Ralph Barton Berry, *Present Philosophical Tendencies: A Critical Survey of Naturalism, Idealism, Pragmatism, and Realism with a Synopsis of the Philosophy of William James* (New York: Longmans, Green & Co., 1912), pp. 158–62.

17. George Berkeley, *A Treatise Concerning the Principles of Human Knowledge* (London: Printed for Jacob Tonson, 1734), Part I, sec. 3, p. 38.

18. Josiah Royce, *The Religious Aspects of Philosophy: A Critique of the Bases of Conduct and of Faith* (Boston: Houghton Mifflin Co., 1885), pp. 441–42, and also, *The World and the Individual*, p. 425, where Royce states: "All things always work together for good from the divine point of view. . . ."

19. Calkins, op. cit., pp. 450–51.

20. Perry, *Journal of Philosophy, Psychology, and Scientific Methods*, VIII, No. 1, 14.

II. *Realism and Pragmatism: The Problem of True Knowledge*

In his paper entitled "Professor Royce's Refutation of Realism and Pluralism," Perry put into print for the first time the statements of what were to become the basic problems and theses of New Realism. In this critique of Royce, Perry offered the following definition of realism which he considered "to be representative of both philosophical realism and common sense. . . . "

The realist believes reality to be a *datum, a somewhat that is given independently of whatever ideas may be formed about it.* According to the realist, the real has a *locus,* a *habitat,* whether or no within some individual experience. Here the real primarily *is,* and is, regardless of whatever secondary meanings, symbols, names, relations or ideas of any kind may be referred to it. The realist conceives of a *thing, and thought about that thing.* They are two orders, not necessarily two kinds; for the thing may be a thought. But in every case the thing of

the first order is indifferent, as far as its being is con-
concerned, to the thought of the second order; which may
reveal but does not constitute or create its object.[1]

The concern of the philosopher, on this account, is not to
define reality but to further efforts to know reality. In fact,
Perry stated in another place that he did "not feel at all sure
that the words 'being' and 'reality' mean anything in exact
discourse." [2] That is to say, that it is only in vain that one
attempts to define reality for "a definition that contains the
term to be defined is of course no definition at all; and every
definition must contain the existential predicate." [3]

Thus, it is seen that the New Realist had a different
philosophical bias from that of the idealist. Montague described
New Realism as "a declaration of independence that would
make it possible to investigate the nature of things on their
own merits without dragging in the tedious and usually
irrelevant fact that they could be experienced by us." [4] While
the idealist would explain the world away in one artfully
contrived picture of systematic unity, the New Realist would
seek to discover the world as it is in all its apparent pluralisms
and apparent contradictions.

The central assumption of the New Realist position derives
from the common sense notion that if one is aware of some
thing, there must *first* be the thing there of which he is aware.
The New Realist insisted upon this notion, but he did not
prove it conclusively because to do so would have involved
him in the same Ego-Centric Predicament which destroyed
the idealist "proof." He did, however, proceed in the attempt
to discover just what was involved in this assumption. He
attempted to follow the lines from this common sense notion

to an expanded conception of the person and personality, the role of consciousness and the workings of consciousness, and its function in the mediation of the objects or things—for the person or personality.

The publications of the several men who wrote in this vein gained in frequency as the first decade of this century wore on. And so did the critical reviews. In 1910 there appeared the first co-operative venture in New Realism, "The Program and Platform of Six Realists." [5] This was followed in 1912 by *The New Realism*.[6] It is significant to note that in these co-operative efforts one might have expected the philosophy of New Realism to take shape as a *philosophy*, but such was not the case. These efforts took the form of individual statements and essays rather than that of the collaborative authorship of a jointly held position. Still, in his *Present Philosophical Tendencies* Perry examined and classified various approaches to philosophy in the interest of advancing New Realism as a philosophy.[7] Indeed, from the very inception of his professional career it is evident that he was working toward the development of just such a realistic philosophy.[8]

Aside from the fact that the New Realists were never fully united except in their rejection of idealism,[9] there was also a problem on the solution to which they were divided. And this problem was crucial to a realistic conception of knowledge. If ideas are dependent on things, then how is one to account for the hallucination or the mirage? Perry is generally considered to have held to that solution which appeared to have dismissed the problem.[10] (His position will be examined in a moment.) While the New Realists, according to Perry, "argued for the immediate presence . . . of physical existence in perception," the Critical Realists (who came on the scene in 1920 with *Essays in Critical Realism*),[11] maintained that "all that one can directly grasp in intuition is *what* the object is, if there is such an object; while *whether* there is such an object or not, can only be taken on 'faith,' or ascertained pragmatically." [12] As Passmore noted, "The original group disintegrated and . . . the contributions to *Contemporary American Philosophy* bear such titles as 'problematic realism,' 'personal realism,' 'empirical idealism,' 'temperamental realism.' " [13] By the thirties the controversies over realism had died down, at least in print, and realism seemed a dead issue.

For Perry, though, realism had not lost its appeal. From the vantage point of middle age he confessed, "When, for the purposes of recovering the past, I re-read my earliest writings, they impress me as extremely convincing, affording an unexpected confirmation of my present philosophical bias." [14] His bias of 1930 was essentially the same as it had been in his earlier years.

Perry attempted to extricate himself from the problems of error and hallucination in the following terms:

> Knowledge is always of an object other than the knowing act. When the object of knowledge reveals itself upon reflection to be distorted, displaced, or otherwise contaminated by the act of knowledge, the second act of knowledge which takes its place extricates itself from *its* object. The correction of knowledge is a perpetual purging away of its own subjectivity. Even when subjectivity itself is known, it becomes object. The last word of a knowing subject—its final deliverance, its statement—uttered or implicit, is object; and not either itself or a relation of object to itself.[15]

Explicit in this statement is the assertion that there are things of which one has knowledge. Yet it is admitted implicitly that there may be error in the immediate perception of things and that correction is often necessary. The blame for such error is, in the passage reproduced above, placed in the act of knowledge. The act of knowledge, according to Perry's argument as examined previously with regard to the Ego-Centric Predicament, is a relationship involving an ego and an object. Interpreting the above passage in relation to the problem of hallucination, a hallucination may be blamed on distortions in the relationship between an ego and the world of things. Such distortions may be of a merely mechanical sort as E. B. Holt pointed out when he compared the lens of the camera and the lens of the eye.[16] Or, they may be of a different sort wherein some such thing as imagination comes more into play. Yet, to say that such things are involved in distortion is to say nothing about how any individual is to know at any given time whether his perception involves the "immediate presence of physical existence."

To talk about the correction of knowledge is only to admit that what was at one time taken to be knowledge was not. It is an admission of error. To say that correction takes place upon reflection that what was taken to be knowledge was not, is to say nothing about the process of such correction. There are still other factors to be considered in the statement under examination.

One of these is the notion of common sense. Whether or not it can ever be proved that there are real things, one must act as though there were. It is reasonable to infer that it was the common sense notion of squaring belief with reality that accounted for Perry's remarks regarding the correction of knowledge. The following tends to support such an inference.

Early in his career Perry stated that the practical man "must recognize in philosophy a kind of reflection that differs only in extent and persistence from the reflection that guides and justifies his life." If philosophy, for Perry, was thought about life, *"thought about the universe in its totality, or in its deepest and essential character . . . ,"* if "such thought, the activity and results was philosophy . . . ," it was thought conceived on the model of common sense realism. It tended to be more rigorous, thorough and technical, but it was conceived on that model.[17]

Common sense is a particularly hazy concept. All sorts of claims are made and purported to be justified by common sense. At times it seems to refer to the uncommon sense of an individual who sees as clear what others do not see at all. At other times it may be taken to refer to the unquestioned, or perhaps, unquestionable (for them) beliefs of a given group of individuals. Common sense realism to Perry refers to the necessary practical belief of men in the existence of the world of people and things.

It would seem then, that Perry's solution to the problems of error and hallucination proceeded along the lines of pragmatism. Yet this was not the whole of his solution nor was it the whole of his realism. Since, however, there was this pragmatic element in Perry's proposed solution, we shall continue the examination in relation to pragmatism.

Perry and Pragmatism—James and Dewey

In having chosen the way of James, Perry did not thereby subscribe *in toto* to the Jamesian view of philosophy. That there was a pragmatic component in Perry's realism does not mean that Perry subscribed fully to the Jamesian conception of pragmatism. Indeed, as early in his career as the presentation of the doctoral dissertation Perry criticized as distortions certain aspects of James' interpretation of Peirce's pragmatism.[18] Yet there were features of James' philosophy with regard to the examination of the notions of mind and of cognition which Perry took over and developed.

One might have noted by this juncture, that some of the issues and controversies in which these men were embroiled have long since died out. Perhaps this is due in part to the success of these men in overcoming opposition to their work. James fought not only in behalf of an interpretation of mind and of reflection, but also for permission to examine such notions. That a mind may be both subject and object of examination, that is, that mind may endeavor to understand mind, does not seem quite so difficult a notion to entertain today as it was at the end of the last century.[19] And yet, the impact of the concluding portion of Perry's "Ego-Centric Predicament" was directed toward advancing the respectability of just such endeavors.

On this point common sense realism and philosophical realism must be distinguished. The respectability of the James-Perry approach was based upon common-sense realism—the sort of realism implicit in such a statement as 'Let's be realistic about the matter,' or 'Let's look at things as they really are.' They sought from this a world-view taken from the world rather than imposed upon the world. Philosophical realism involved the assertion that a world-view conceived through the model of common-sense investigation was the only legitimate world-view. It was in the construction of this position, oddly enough, that realism seems to have left the realm of common sense.

One may begin the examination of this contention with the notion of "pure experience." James set this forth in the following:

> By the term "pure" prefixed to the word "experience" I mean to denote a form of being which is as yet neutral

or ambiguous, and prior to the object and the subject distinction, I mean to show that the attribution either of physical or mental being to an experience is due to nothing in the immediate stuff of which the experience is composed—for the same stuff will serve for either attribution—but rather to two contrasted groups of associates with either of which . . . our reflection . . . tends to connect it. . . . Functioning in the whole context of our experience in one way, an experience figures as a mental fact. Functioning in another way, it figures as a physical object. In itself it is actually neither but virtually both.[20]

The notion of a "neutral being" is rather puzzling from the point of view of common sense. To speak of the attribution of mental or physical being suggests at the very least that there is something that does the attributing and that "mental being" or "physical being" is dependent upon being so conceived by someone. Since conception is a cognitive relation, it seems, then, that whether an experience is connected with the mind or the physical world is dependent upon a subject's cognitive activity.

But this does not mean that such a cognitive activity makes things real or unreal. One must consider the problem of the "ambiguity of a set of words used to refer to the transactions between the mind and its environment. The same word is used sometimes for the mental act, sometimes for its object and sometimes for both." Thus, for example, experience "may be taken to mean the act of experiencing or *what* is experienced, or the total process or relationship in which somebody experiences something." [21]

The point here, according to Perry at least, is that James was not referring to being or to stuff at all. He did not mean to denote a form of neutral being in his notion of pure experience, but was concerned with neutral terms. Perry stated this as follows:

> In so far as I divide them into elements, the contents of my mind exhibit no generic character. I find the quality 'blue,' but this I ascribe also to the book . . . on the table . . . , the elements of the introspective manifold are in themselves neither peculiarly mental nor peculiarly mine; they are *neutral and interchangeable.*[22]

When consciousness is subjected to the experimentalist test, it is no longer an unanalyzable and self-revealing entity. It becomes a function or relationship of terms which in themselves are consciousless and which, because they are free from any advanced commitment to either the mental or the physical forms of complexity into which they *may* enter, are said to be neutral.[23]

This conception of neutrality applies to the problem of hallucination in the following manner. The individual in experiencing the hallucination has more than a bare experience. Whether he will tend to connect it with the physical or mental world depends upon the whole context of his experiences. James put this forth in the following:

> Perception is not of instant and isolated presentation— a discontinuous series of pebbles, or beats, or bolts—each complete in itself. It is pervaded throughout by ulterior reference, by pointing, by a sense of more to come. The object of perception is always something demanded by what has gone before and demanding a sequel. It fills a place in a context which surrounds it like a fringe.[24]

The individual has a history as a person which tends to color the way in which he categorizes his experiences. It is important to point out also that in the process of acquiring his history the individual is involved in the taking over of part of the history of those with whom he comes in contact in the groups to which he belongs. That an imaginary monster is real to the child in a way that it is not to the parent, may be explained by the difference in their histories with regard to this categorization. Further, the common sense relegation of such a monster to the realm of the mind on the part of the adult is a consequence of his instruction in such matters in the historical process of developing his own person.

But this does not say anything with regard to the reality of the existence of the monster. That the child may be prone to call it real and the adult to call it false suggests that all reality is a matter of naming things real or otherwise. However, Perry maintained his conviction that one was still limited by reality as to what could be called real. His position was as follows:

> The function of knowing mind must be conceived so as to provide for its ultimate objectivity. At the same time that it makes a difference, it must take things as they are. The only way to resolve this seeming paradox is to conceive knowing as an external-relation—that is, a relation which is added to or superimposed upon what *was* already, in its absence. Such an external relation is provided by the function of selection. What is selected is there to be selected, and is not instituted by the act of selection. Being selected, it acquires not only that new role, but new cross-relationships to the jointly selected and the non-selected. A new boundary is drawn having its within and without. Relations of pattern,

fusion, perspective, and contrast arise—whatever relations, in short, follow from being included together and included exclusively.[25]

The hallucination, then, may be explained in these relationships as they arise for a given individual or even given individuals together in accordance with their selection from reality. This does not mean, however, that the object ostensibly perceived exists as such in reality. Rather it means that there could be no such hallucination without some reality from which it or its components could be selected. But this is something else than an argument "for the immediate presence . . . of physical existence in perception." Indeed, it is more in accord with the view of the Critical Realists as Perry characterized it. Perry appears to have come around to the following view which, as he showed, stemmed from James:

That which mind selects and which thereby becomes its object or content is acted *on* and *with*; it becomes the occasion and the instrument of causal operations which induce changes in the environment of future action. Selection thus provides an explanation, not only of the realism of knowledge—its submission to the facts as it finds them—but also of the idealism of knowledge—that is, the novelty which it introduces. At the same time it provides for the factor of interest and unites James' radical empiricism with his pragmatism. For selection is dictated by the subject's needs, desires, and purposes. It isolates and takes account of that which is relevant to practice.[26]

Perry thus held that one takes account of what is relevant to practice. The consideration whether the individual who has a hallucination is involved in this sort of thing lies in the realm of psychology and is not pursued any further. Without attempting to prejudice such inquiry, though, it is suggested that the so-called normal person in our society is one who discounts the hallucination as irrelevant or as deleterious to practical activity. However, this raises other questions with regard to the concept of normality and with regard to what might be practical for the so-called abnormal individual.

While Perry appears to have taken over this Jamesian conception of the interplay of the idealism and realism of knowledge, he still maintained his position of what may be termed 'hard core realism.' To understand this fact one must examine more closely what did and did not appeal to him in pragmatism.

The pragmatist theory of knowledge, according to Perry, represented a particular kind of answer to two questions: "first, what is the role of ideas in knowledge? second, what is the difference between a true idea and a false idea?" [27]

On the pragmatic view an idea performs the function of representing or meaning a particular experience. Naturally, it is not the same as that experience nor does it resemble its object any more than the word 'horse' resembles a horse. However, it does permit abstraction and therefore serves as a sort of "intellectual currency" which permits thinking about things. "More specifically, an idea means a thing when it projects a series of acts that would, if carried out, bring that thing into the same immediacy which the idea already enjoys. The virtue of ideas thus lies primarily in their being practical substitutes for immediacy." [28] Of course, in the process of abstraction something of the experience to which it refers has been left out, but to the extent that this fact is not ignored, so that the abstraction is not imputed to be the whole of the experience, it need not be misleading.

Pragmatism's answer to the second question, according to Perry, is as follows:

> For pragmatism . . . truth does not mean the same thing as reality or existence, but is a property, exclusively, of that instance of existence which we call 'idea' or 'belief' in its relation to that second instance of reality or existence which we call 'object' of the first. Truth is a property of ideas as these arise amid the actual processes of human thinking; it is something which happens to ideas in the course of their natural history. . . .
> *An idea is true when it works; that is, when it is successful, when it fulfills its function, or performs what is demanded of it.* An idea is essentially *for* something; and when it does what it is *for*, it is the 'right' or the 'true' idea.[29]

As Perry noted, however, there are various uses which ideas may serve. The question thus arises as to whether there is not a difference in the nature of the types of verification of ideas and the priority of these types in situations where they conflict. Perry categorized these modes of verification as *"verification by perception, consistency, operation, sentiment,* and *general utility."* [30]

Verification by perception means, simply, following up the meaning of an idea in the attempt to recover its object. If the perception is what was to be expected, the idea is true. If, on the other hand, a sense of surprise or shock of novelty rather than a sense of recognition occurs, then the idea is false. Verification by consistency refers to the "testing of an idea on trial, by ideas already in good and regular standing. The idea is proved true by this test when it is not contradicted by other ideas, or is positively implied by them." [31]

These two modes of verification "correspond to the traditional criteria of empiricism and rationalism." Perry advocated that, in the interest of clarity, "the term 'true' [be] restricted to ideas verified in one of these ways. . . . "[32] For, while he granted that alternative theories may be equally compatible with all our knowledge, and that we choose between them for subjective reasons or subsequential utility, he would prefer that the validation of such a choice "remain as extra-logical grounds of belief. One might readily agree that truth in this narrower sense [restriction to these forms of verification] was an insufficient criterion, that the exigencies of life required belief in excess of proof. But the stricter truth tests would not be confused nor their priority compromised."[33]

Perry's position on this matter becomes clearer in his examination of verification by operation. Here he meant the same thing as James' subsequential utility. In Perry's words, "my idea of my future state is verified in this sense in so far as the plans which I base on it succeed."[34] Theoretical truths are often such as have bearing or implication on the practical side of life, as for example the truths of physical science. But he denied that such practicality is an independent test of truth. Rather, it uses the "familiar tests of experiment and inference" in the process of determining the practicality of a course of action.[35] Thus, for example, the determination of the utility of a physical theory for the building of bridges is a matter of experiment and reason involving verification both by consistency and with perception. The answer to the question 'will it work?' is itself dependent upon such verification.

Verification by sentiment raises even further difficulties regarding the notion of a practical criterion of truth. Here the test seems to be pleasantness or peace of mind or making life worth living. Perry noted that such considerations are allowed by both James and Schiller to have weight only in situations where "the tests of perception and consistency are not decisive . . . The perfectly agreeable hypothesis must yield at once before fact or contradiction." [36] Perry did recognize that in such things as religion or faith, for example, such proof is impossible and that at times we "must in the practical sense believe where we cannot in the theoretical sense know." [37] Moreover, as James pointed out in his *Will to Believe*,[38] there are occasions when belief on the part of an actively engaged person might be the decisive factor in bringing about the facts that prove the belief true. The presence of a belief as an emotional charge or spur to action may make all the difference between success or failure in one's endeavors. But the truth of the belief is determined by subsequent events seen in the light not of sentiment but of the basic criteria of verification.

The final criterion of verification listed by Perry was that of general utility—"the proof of an idea's truth by the total satisfaction it affords, by its suitability to all the purposes of life, individual and social." [39] Such a criterion is not really allowed by James and Dewey, according to Perry, because of their contention that "the truth of an idea is determined by the specific purpose and the specific situation that give rise to the idea." [40] In Dewey's words: "It is the failure to grasp the coupling of truth of meaning with a specific *promise*, undertaking or intention expressed by a thing which underlies, so far as I can see, the criticisms passed upon the experimental or pragmatic view of the truth." [41] Perry opposed the criterion of general utility just because it tends to blur the distinctions and priorities of the individual criteria of verification already considered. This blurring is considered dangerous because it seems, despite the Deweyan disclaimer, to encourage the equalization of all of these criteria as valid criteria for determining verification. This is tantamount to encouraging the notion, for example, that the criterion of sentiment is just as good a criterion of truth as that of perception. This, as has been noted, Perry could not accept.

His position thus far is summarized in the following passage:

> There remains a strict and limited pragmatism which is not guilty of this offense. Such a pragmatism consists in the proof that the theoretic interest itself is in fact an interest. Ideas are functional rather than substantial. Their relation to their object is not one of resemblance, but of leading or guidance. Their verification is not a matching of similars, but a process in which their leading or guidance is followed to that terminus of fact or being which they mean. And since the theoretic interest *is* an interest, it is as a whole rooted in life, and answerable to the needs and projects of life. In other words, truth, a theoretic utility, has also, because of the auspices under which it is begotten, a subsequential utility. Finally, it is the proper and consistent sequel to this to allow taste, aspiration, and hope to incline the balance of belief when, and only when, truth in the strict sense is not attainable.[42]

In this attempt at squaring Perry's realism with his pragmatism it is not necessary to go into the metaphysical implications of the latter, for, as Perry noted, one may be either an idealist sort or realist sort of pragmatist in outlook. Consequently, his arguments with regard to realism and idealism are more to the point than arguments concerning pragmatic metaphysics. Indeed, he maintained, in effect, that pragmatism could be no more than a theory of knowledge if it was to avoid relativism or an absolutist metaphysic which would take it beyond its cherished empirical and naturalistic limits.[43]

Yet, even as a theory of knowledge pragmatism was not wholly satisfactory to Perry. Some of these points of dissatisfaction have already been considered. The common thread that runs through them is their identification of truth with that which satisfies the individual confronted by puzzling situations. Perry objected to Dewey's statement that, "What we want is something that takes itself as knowledge, rightly or wrongly." [44] Perry considered this to be more properly conceived as *"arriving at belief"* [45] rather than arriving at truth. It was this type of extension of Peirce's operationalism to which Perry objected as early as the presentation of his doctoral dissertation.[46] If the pragmatic theory of truth is strictly held to be no more than is apparent in Dewey's statement, it is on this view incompatible with realism. "The pragmatist insists that true knowledge is a function of the process of knowledge. The critic of pragmatism insists, firstly, that true knowledge is also a function of the thing known; secondly, that in this latter functional relation is to be found the element of truth. Truth, because it is part of the cognitive interest, must satisfy; but because it is *truth* it must envisage reality." [47]

Perry's realism may now be summarized in the following manner. First, it represented a rejection of idealism whether in its relativist or absolutist forms. Second, it was an assertion that, at bottom, ideas are dependent upon things and not the reverse. Third, it embodied an acceptance of the pragmatic explanation of arriving at belief coupled with the common sense notion of the correction of belief in terms of perception of reality. Finally, it provided for the possibility of the correction of belief arising from error in perception and explained error in perception, both, in pragmatic terms. Pragmatism was to serve the realistic theory of knowledge and was not permitted any method of determining truth which claimed parity with or superiority to the realistic methods of experiment and inference, that is, verification by perception and consistency.

Pragmatism in its emphasis on the need of the individual for the attainment of belief had yet another influence on Perry. Dewey was concerned with *"social philosophy and progress,* thought consisting in the perpetual reconstruction of ends or purposes by which the life of the group is liberalized and expanded."[48] So too was Perry interested in progress and the liberalized and expanded life. His concern, however, was expressed in terms of his realism.

Perry's Realism, Theory of Value, and Theory of Society

John Passmore in his remarks regarding the decline in the vigor of New Realism noted that with the disintegration of the original group of American New Realists Perry became a moral theorist and scholar.[49] Perry did indeed concern himself most specifically with moral and social philosophy during and after the twenties until his death in 1957. It is important to recall that he did so as a New Realist. Certainly he felt that his work in these areas was intimately bound up with his New Realism, as has already been indicated in the quotation from his personal statement which was written six years after the publication of his *General Theory of Value*. Furthermore, his interest in moral and social philosophy was a major feature of his career from its very inception and was an important part of his New Realism. Witness the very title of his doctoral dissertation, "The Life of Reflection and Energy: An Ethical Defense of the Common Morality of Freedom, Duty and Goodness."[50] It included the following passages:

> The actor, viewing his deed as an actual one from a possible many, propounds to himself the query: Why this rather than another? Reason is born with the question "why?" When it was first uttered the world became

rational and when it was first applied to conduct the world became moral.[51]

There is only one important question in the world, to wit: What should I do? Man may think or not as he pleases but act he must. As life is the one indisputable fact, so the manner of life is the one unavoidable problem.[52]

It was his emphasis upon the *fact* of life which, as was noted earlier, helps to explain his rejection of idealism. It was his insistence on the individual's need to act and to take account of reality and real consequence in pursuing his actions which constituted the realistic basis of his morality. Perry was concerned throughout his career to place the moral question squarely on the shoulders of man. Under the chapter heading "A Realistic Philosophy of Life" in *Present Philosophical Tendencies,* he stated as follows:

Life has maintained itself, and promoted its interests, in proportion as it has become aware of the actual character of its environment. It is the practical function of intelligence, not to read goodness into the facts, but to lay bare the facts in all their indifference and brutality; so that action may be contrived to fit them, to the end that goodness may prevail.[53]

The term 'interests' here is of crucial importance. It provides the key to Perry's social and moral philosophy as well as the main link from these to his realistic epistemology. The notion of interest accounted for the idealism of knowledge in selection from reality. It represented for Perry what was valuable in pragmatic theory in accounting for arrival at belief. It made no claim to the title of source of final truth in and of itself. Rather it was derived from an examination of the subject in the cognitive relation with reality. It represented the fruit of Perry's endeavor to take this subject and make of it an object of knowledge. That is, Perry endeavored to look at man in realistic terms and found him to be at bottom an interested animal.

Thus Perry had taken his cue from James whom he credited with holding as his object "man the organism, saving [*sic*] himself and asserting his interests within the natural environment. These interests . . . must be the centre and point of reference in any account of mind." [54] Perry stated that "content of mind must be defined *as that portion of the surrounding environment which is taken account of by the organism in serving its interests,* the nervous system, physiologically regarded, being the mechanism which is employed." [55] It is worth noting that in Perry's terms this was not only a "physiological account of the action of the mind" but also a "moral account."

But what made it a moral account in Perry's view? In the following passage his answer was clear in placing interest at the root of his moral and social philosophy:

> Nature, as interpreted for common sense by the inorganic sciences, presents a spectacle of impassivity. There is neither fortune nor calamity, neither comedy nor tragedy, because no claims are made. . . . But with the addition of life, the whole situation must be reconstructed. The organism inherits the earth, and the varieties of nature become the resources of the vital interest. The vital interest acts upon the environment in its own behalf, thus transmuting material existence into value. . . . The realm of natural life, embracing innumerable desires externally related and struggling for the possession

of material resources, constitutes a new order in which good and evil abound. Morality arises only when there is such dividing and compounding of interests as to permit of some interplay of part interests and whole interests, of exclusiveness and considerateness. The moral being appears as one divided against himself; as one uniting interests into a self, varying from a desultory collection to an absorbing purpose; or as one brought to recognize the claims of a community.[56]

Thus the notion of interest is the key to Perry's theory of value and theory of society. This notion is now to be set out in more detail in the examination of these theories.

1. Ralph Barton Perry, "Professor Royce's Refutation of Realism and Pluralism," *Monist*, XII, No. 3 (1902), 450–51.

2. Ralph Barton Perry, "The Ego Centric Predicament," *Journal of Philosophy, Psychology, and Scientific Methods*, VIII, No. 1 (1910), 7.

3. Perry, *Monist*, loc. cit., p. 447.

4. William Pepperell Montague, "Confessions of an Animistic Materialist," *Contemporary American Philosophy: Personal Statements*, ed. George P. Adams and William Pepperell Montague (2 vols.; New York: Macmillan Co., 1930), II, p. 145.

5. Edwin B. Holt et al., "The Program and Platform of Six Realists," *Journal of Philosophy, Psychology, and Scientific Methods*, Vol. VII, No. 15 (1910).

6. Edwin B. Holt et al., *The New Realism: Co-operative Studies in Philosophy* (New York: Macmillan Co., 1912).

7. Ralph Barton Perry, *Present Philosophical Tendencies: A Critical Survey of Naturalism, Idealism, Pragmatism, and Realism with a Synopsis of the Philosophy of William James* (New York: Longmans, Green & Co., 1912), esp. Part V.

8. See Ralph Barton Perry, "The Life of Reflection and Energy: An Ethical Defense of the Common Morality of Freedom, Duty, and Goodness" (Ph.D. diss., Harvard University, 1899).

9. Morris Raphael Cohen, *American Thought: A Critical Sketch* (Glencoe: Free Press, 1954), p. 305, and John Passmore, *A Hundred Years of Philosophy* (New York: Macmillan Co., 1957), p. 263.

10. Passmore, op. cit., pp. 263–64.

11. Durant Drake et al., *Essays in Critical Realism: A Co-operative Study of the Problem of Knowledge* (London: Macmillan and Co., 1920).

12. Alfred Weber, *History of Philosophy*, trans. Frank Thilly, with *Philosophy since 1860* by Ralph Barton Perry (New York: Charles Scribner's Sons, 1925), pp. 590–91.

13. Passmore, op. cit., p. 265 and p. 265 n.

14. Ralph Barton Perry, "Realism in Retrospect," *Contemporary American Philosophy*, II, 187.

15. Ralph Barton Perry, "A Note on Neutralism," *Structure, Method and Meaning: Essays in Honor of Henry M. Sheffer*, ed. Paul Henle, Horace M. Kallen, and Susan K. Langer (New York: Liberal Arts Press, 1951), pp. 222–23.

16. Edwin B. Holt, "The Place of Illusory Experience in a Realistic World," *The New Realism*, pp. 304–6.

17. Ralph Barton Perry, *The Approach to Philosophy* (New York: Charles Scribner's Sons, 1905), pp. 21–22.

18. Perry, "The Life of Reflection and Energy," pp. 15–16.

19. See, for example, William James, "A Plea for Psychology as a Natural Science," *Philosophical Review*, I, No. 2 (1892), and also his essay "The Relations between Knower and Known," *The Meaning of Truth* (New York: Longmans, Green & Co., 1909).

20. William James, quoted in Ralph Barton Perry, *The Thought and Character of William James: As Revealed in Unpublished Correspondence and Notes, Together with His Published Writings* (2 vols.; Boston: Little, Brown & Co., 1935). II, 385–86, James's quotes.

21. Perry, "A Note on Neutralism," *Structure, Method, and Meaning*, p. 219; Perry's italics.

22. Perry, *Present Philosophical Tendencies*, p. 277.

23. Perry, "A Note on Neutralism," *Structure, Method, and Meaning*, p. 223.

24. William James, quoted in Perry, *The Thought and Character of William James*, I, 500.

25. Perry, "A Note on Neutralism," *Structure, Method, and Meaning*, loc. cit.

26. Perry, "A Note on Neutralism," *Structure, Method, and Meaning,* pp. 223–24; Perry's italics.

27. Perry, *Present Philosophical Tendencies,* p. 200.

28. Ibid., p. 201, Perry's italics; and cf. James, *The Meaning of Truth,* pp. 30–31, 43–50, and 110.

29. Perry, *Present Philosophical Tendencies,* p. 204; Perry's quotes and italics.

30. Ibid., p. 205.

31. Ibid., pp. 205–6.

32. Ibid., pp. 206–7.

33. Ibid., p. 207.

34. Ibid.

35. Ibid., p. 208.

36. Ibid., p. 210.

37. Ibid.

38. William James, *The Will to Believe and Other Essays in Popular Philosophy* (New York: Longman's, Green & Co., 1927), p. 25: "There are . . . cases where a fact cannot come at all unless a preliminary faith exists in its coming."

39. Perry, *Present Philosophical Tendencies,* p. 211.

40. Ibid.

41. John Dewey, *The Influence of Darwin on Philosophy and Other Essays in Contemporary Thought* (New York: Henry Holt and Co., 1910), p. 5 n.

42. Perry, *Present Philosophical Tendencies,* p. 213; Perry's italics.

43. Ibid., p. 213–21.

44. John Dewey, "The Experimental Theory of Knowledge," *Mind,* N.S., XV, No. 59 (1906), 20.

45. Ralph Barton Perry, "A Review of Pragmatism as a Theory of Knowledge," *Journal of Philosophy, Psychology, and Scientific Methods,* IV, No. 14 (1907), 366.

46. Perry, "The Life of Reflection and Energy," pp. 15–16.

47. Perry, *Journal of Philosophy, Psychology, and Scientific Methods,* IV, No. 14, 374; Perry's italics.

48. Ralph Barton Perry, *Philosophy of the Recent Past: An Outline of European and American Philosophy Since 1860* (New York: Charles Scribner's Sons, 1926), p. 195.

49. Passmore, op. cit., p. 265.

50. Perry, op. cit.

51. Ibid., p. 21; Perry's quotes.

52. Ibid., p. 2.

53. Perry, *Present Philosophical Tendencies*, p. 329.

54. Perry, *Present Philosophical Tendencies*, p. 350, and cf. William James, "Spencer's Definition of Mind," *Journal of Speculative Philosophy*, Vol. XII (January, 1878).

55. Perry, *Present Philosophical Tendencies*, p. 300; Perry's italics.

56. Ralph Barton Perry, "The Conception of Moral Goodness," *Philosophical Review*, XVI, No. 2 (1907), 152–53.

III. Perry's Theory of Value*

Perry's theory of value is summed up in the statement that value is the object of any interest. Interest was taken to be "the original source and constant feature of all value. Any object, whatever it be, acquires [sic] value when any interest whatever it be is taken in it. . . . " While this might have been "value simpliciter—value in the elementary primordial and generic sense," [1] the development, elucidation and defense of the theory involved its author in the most intricate and complex argument and analysis. It is not hard to see why.

Had Perry left no more than this summary statement it would appear surprising, or even disappointing, that he should have proposed such a theory of value. He was supposed to be committed to doing good through philosophy. Yet, was the sum and substance of value to be found in the old saw "one man's

* For the sake of maintaining continuity in what might otherwise appear a somewhat piecemeal approach, it may be helpful to have an overview of the theory in capsule form. Consult the Appendix on page 87 for a summary outline of this chapter, which has been keyed to the enumerated sideheads for easy reference.

meat is another man's poison?" Was theory of value to sink into the mire of *de gustibus non est disputandum?*

Perry did not suffer us to face these questions without instruction. He did not wait for his critics to raise them. The exposition of his theory may be viewed, in part, as an attempt to answer them. It would be most unfair to judge Perry solely on the basis of his summary definition of value. At the same time the intricacy and complexity of his developed position suggest difficulty in judging his theory all at once. In order to avoid over-generalization in judgment whether based upon either too little or too much exposition, a sort of middle course will be steered. Perry's position will be set forth and discussed in stages. This will provide a foundation for the direction of a more general critique.

Before proceeding with the detailed examination of Perry's theory of value, a few words are in order about the two-fold task that Perry had set for himself. He was concerned with both value and obligation. Theory of value and theory of morality, although not the same, are intimately related. As Perry might have put it, the former deals with the applicability of terms 'good,' 'better' and 'best' and their opposites. The latter deals with obligation, the rightness or wrongness of action, what ought or ought not to be done. The intimacy of their relationship is exposed in the translation of degrees of 'rightness' in such questions as, 'Is it good that I do this?' 'Is it better to do this than that?' 'What is the best course to follow?' The problem of morality contains within it the problem of value. As Perry viewed them such questions as these represent requests for knowledge of value.

The impact of Perry's position is to break down the barriers between theory of value and theory of morality. The search for moral knowledge becomes the search for knowledge of value and *vice versa*. What would have made these moral questions, for Perry, was that knowledge of value was to serve as the source of obligation. He insisted that "what one ought to do is not simply what one wants to do; it must be proved to be right or the best. . . . " [2] Morality, for Perry, required doing what is right and what is good because it is right and good. The question of obligation boils down to a consideration of the effects of following or not following particular courses of action. A general theory of value would not be general if it could not speak with equal voice to ethics as well as aesthetics, for example. It was precisely this ideal that Perry wished to serve in the construction of his theory of value.

This does not mean that theory of value and theory of morality are equated in all respects. Thus, for example, ethics and aesthetics are still different at least in that they refer to different ranges of cases and contexts for the application of theory of value. This is what Perry meant by *Realms of Value*. It is significant, however, that the person who functions in accordance with the principles of this theory of value is, in so doing, a moral person by definition. Far from indicating a defect in the position now to be examined, this may appear in the last analysis as a point in its favor.

A. *Value Theories Rejected*

The influence of James' critical common-sensism on Perry cannot be overstated. This is not to say that the latter became a mere disciple, promulgating and interpreting the words of the master to the masses. Had Perry become this and no more, he would have betrayed rather than honored his master. For it was not so much a body of doctrines that made a mark on Perry, as a set of attitudes which would permit no blind acceptance of dogma and insisted on the right and the responsibility of the individual for the critical examination of issues and positions on issues in the light of experience. This set of attitudes served both as the touchstone for Perry's critique of other theories of value and as the cornerstone of his own theory. He exulted in the right and accepted the responsibility and found that those theories to which he turned his attention had been so devised as to defy such criticism. His theory of value was intended not to defy but to withstand such criticism.

He rejected those theories which depended upon mystical elements for their cohesiveness. Whether value was held to stem from a divine super-human authority as a God or from a pseudo-divine supra-human authority as a society, Perry's attack was essentially the same. Such authorities are untestable by their very natures. To posit a mind of God or a mind of society as the source of value is in effect to assert and not prove that the individual man has no hand in the business of determining or checking values. His duty is to accept and obey. Perry asked how anyone could know there is a mind of God or of society. Mind, on Perry's view presumed an organism. Society, by definition is a group of organisms. A group as such does not will or think; its members will and think.[3]

His attack on inspiration, revelation, and intuition followed in the same vein. These are all essentially untestable. They represent the claim of an individual to private access to the truth. One either gets the message or he does not. Why should anyone who did not get the message believe the person who claims he did get the message and/or follow the 'word'? What if intuitions conflict? Whose 'truth' does one follow?[4] And it is the question of truth which is all important.

It is the obscurity involved in the various value theories to which Perry objected. He flayed the circuitous word games of the idealists, as asserting no more than the maxim, " 'I ought to do whatever I ought to do when I feel truly.' " He complained that no matter how many terms such as "Absolute judgment, . . . eternal, standard, universal, necessary, objective, or consistent . . . " are used to qualify 'truly,' nothing is gained that distinguishes feeling truly from feeling falsely. As a consequence obligation remains "a wholly individual and capricious matter." Even Kant's injunction to "act on a maxim that thou canst will to be law universal" was reduced by Perry to the statement that "you ought to do what you truly ought to do." [5] Perry's point was not just that it did not resolve the practical problem of determining how one would know what he truly ought to do, but more important that it merely repeated a problem while pretending to be a solution.

Again, in dealing with the position of G. E. Moore, he attacked the obscurities of intuitionism for similar reasons. The very presumption that good was some sort of unanalyzable simple quality apprehended intuitively was unintelligible to Perry. That one could perceive something as good analogously to one's perception of its being yellow strained his realism just a bit too hard. Perry attacked the position on the grounds that such a quality would then somehow have to be in objects empirically. As he put it:

There is no difficulty over the meaning of terms connoting empirical qualities, nor is there serious difference of opinion as to their distribution. Things wear them in public, and any passer-by may note them. But no one who has read Mr. Moore's solemn observations concerning what things are or are not good, can for an instant be deceived into supposing that his perception has lit upon a quality whose evident presence he reports for our benefit.[6]

The issue was not whether Moore was an empiricist but whether his analogy drawn from the world of real things had anything to offer to people involved in the world of real things. Did it offer truth in place of confusion, or more scholarly confusion in place of less scholarly confusion?

Even the pragmatist Dewey was guilty in Perry's eyes of confounding while ostensibly elucidating the topic of value. Dewey's treatment of value judgment was unacceptable to him in that it failed to maintain the distinction between valuing and judging. This was an extension of the issue between them over the relativism of knowledge and truth.

Dewey emphasized the distinction between what someone wants and what he ought to want, between what he desires and that which is worthy of his desire. His position is illustrated in the following:

> To say that something satisfies is to report something as an isolated finality. To assert that it is satis*factory* is to define it in its connections and interactions. The fact that it pleases or is immediately congenial poses a problem to judgment. How shall the satisfaction be rated? Is it a value or is it not? Is it something to be prized and cherished, *to be* enjoyed? Not stern moralists alone but everyday experience informs us that finding satisfaction in a thing may be a warning, a summons to be on the lookout for consequences. To declare something satis*factory* is to assert that it meets specifiable conditions. It is, in effect, a judgment that the thing "will do." It involves a prediction: it contemplates a future in which the thing will continue to serve; it *will* do. It asserts a consequence the thing will actively institute; it will *do*. That it is

satisfying is the content of a proposition of fact; that it is satisfactory is a judgment, an estimate, an appraisal. It denotes an attitude *to be* taken, that of striving to perpetuate and to make secure.[7]

Now, this suggests that value is created in the process of judging value. The judgment that something will do in the future is a judgment that one will continue to so judge in the future. In effect, Dewey's value judgment is the judgment of judgment of value. If judgment is itself colored by individual preferences, Dewey's position becomes hopelessly confused. It cannot explain how judgment creates value because of its assertion, in effect, that value plays a part in judgment and in the definition of the truth of that judgment. As Perry saw it, such a position represented a maze leading nowhere rather than a gateway to understanding. He noted that "to say that an object is valuable when it is judged to be valuable, appears to be either viciously or sceptically relative, if all judgments are accepted; or merely redundant if only *true* judgments are accepted. In the latter case one virtually says that an object is valuable when it is in fact valuable." [8]

The problem of relativism presented a challenge to Perry. Each of the views that he scrutinized represented a dogmatic denial of the relativism of value or else could be reduced to that extreme view which he characterized as vicious or extreme relativism, the view that both knowledge and value are relative to desire. Perry sought to avoid the pitfalls at either extreme. The heart of his position is contained in the following:

It is entirely conceivable that the *value* of *a* should consist in its being desired; in other words, in that specific relationship which the desiderative consciousness supplies or superadds to the object a. We should then say that the being or nature of things is independent of their possessing value, but not that *their possessing value* is independent of consciousness. . . . [9]

Thus to know a is to create neither a's existence nor a's value. To desire a is (conceivably) to create a's value. The relativism of value refers to the individual desiring person as the creator of value. It is on this foundation that Perry sought to construct a theory in which "the relativism of value loses those characters of arbitrariness, contradictoriness, and asymmetry, which make it morally and logically objectionable." [10] This was certainly no light task. The notion of a "desiderative consciousness" had to be developed in a fashion that would clarify the relationship between knowledge and desire and still avoid the obscurity of Dewey's 'value-judgment.' This development proceeded with the introduction of the terms 'interest' and 'object.'

B. *Value as the Object of Any Interest*

When Perry stated that it was "entirely conceivable that the value of a should consist in its being desired . . . ," he was not linking value unequivocally to desire. The force of the qualification "entirely conceivable" was to indicate that desire might be only one aspect of a more fundamental concept. This concept was interest. As he put it, "X is valuable $=$ interest is taken in X." [11] The relationships remained the same. Interest did not create its object, X. Interest involved a function of an individual with respect to its object. Perry summarized his intentions in the following:

> In short, interest being constitutive of value in the basic sense, theory of value will take this as its point of departure and centre of reference; and will classify and systematize values in terms of the different forms which interest and their objects may be found to assume.[12]

Perry's first step in this job of classification and systematization was to develop the basic meaning of 'interest' and 'object' in order to clarify the relationships between them. As will be seen, 'interest' was grounded in his view of the nature of man and 'object' was grounded in his realism.

1. *Interest and Perry's view of man.*—Without mentioning Perry by name, but leaving no doubts that it was Perry's theory to which he referred, John Dewey castigated a theory of value based on interest as stemming from introspectionist psychology.[13] Yet Perry's bias in psychological theory was, if anything, toward behaviorism. He wished to "look for interest in the open—upon the plane and in the context of physical nature." [14] Still, introspectionism played a prominent part in his theory of value, but not as the means for the establishment of interest as the source of value.

He defined interest as a *"state, act, attitude or disposition of favor or disfavor. . . . "* He stated, "It is characteristic of living mind to be *for* some things and *against* others. . . . To be 'for' or 'against' is to view with favor or disfavor. . . . " It was this characteristic "bias of the subject toward or away from," to which he gave the name 'interest.' [15] On this point, that to have interests is inherent in the nature of man, Perry claimed an empirical basis for his theory of value.

He took pains to provide evidence from the fields of biology, physiology and psychology to support the contention that men do in fact have such dispositions.[16] Some of these are common to all men and are very much like instincts, in the way that they influence activity for self-preservation and the propagation of the species. Some interests are dispositions to react in particular ways to external stimuli; others are dispositions to react in particular ways to certain bio-physical internal stimuli.[17] The adaptability of the higher animals, and especially of man, allows for the development of new interests as well as the elimination of old interests.[18] Perry also noted evidence that man has certain governing propensities, or dispositions, which tend to dominate his activities at any given time.[19]

The common thread running through these different sorts of interest is the idea of disposition toward action. Now, one hardly observes disposition in the open. The behaviorist approach involves the identification and presentation of stimuli and the observation of action. Then dispositions may be inferred to account for observed regularities in response to stimuli. While this is an oversimplified view, indeed a caricature, of behaviorism, it does serve to indicate that Perry defined and categorized interest in behavioral terms.

A look at his discussion of the "polarity" of interest will illuminate this point a bit more. "Polarity" referred to "that duality of *for* or *against* which is repeated throughout the whole range of interests in such pairs as desire and aversion, liking and disliking, favor and disfavor." [20] 'For' and 'against' become respectively 'positive' and 'negative.' Now, taking "interested response in the general sense" to mean "performance for the sake of its consequences, or performance determined by what the agent expects as a result of it," Perry defined positive and negative interest as follows: "Positive interest will then be a response determined by a positive expectation; and negative interest a response determined by a negative expectation." [21] The particular conception of expectation here becomes clearer in the light of the following passages:

> Interest is *a train of events determined by expectation of its outcome.* Or, *a thing is an object of interest when its being expected induces actions looking to its realization or non-realization.* Thus peace is an object of interest when acts believed to be conducive to peace, or preventive of peace, are performed on that account, or when events are selected or rejected because peace is expected of them.[22]

> Just as . . . it is the object of expectation which is the object of interest, so . . . it will be the sign of the expectation . . . that defines the sign of the interest.[23]

To speak of interest as "a train of events determined by expectation of its outcome" is to assert *a fortiori* that interest is to be inferred from action. 'Expectation' serves to indicate that interest is not identical with this action. Positive interest is an attitude of favor. It is an inclination to act in behalf of the attainment or achievement of its expected object, or in behalf of the prolongation of the enjoyment of its object. Negative interest is an attitude of disfavor or inclination to destroy its object or to escape from its expected presence. The "term 'good' . . . in the most general sense . . . means the character which anything derives from being the object of positive interest: whatever is desired, liked, enjoyed, willed, or hoped for, is *thereby* good." [24] The term 'bad,' correspondingly means the character anything derives from being the object of a negative interest.[25] The meaning of value is thus derived by inference from behavior.

At this point it is advisable to pause and to consider more clearly what Perry meant by 'man' having interests. Although it is convenient to use such an omnibus term as 'man' in speaking about characteristics of human beings, it should not be forgotten that such a 'man' is not an existent entity. While in discourse it is made to take the place of individual human beings, it is important to remember that only individuals are organisms and can have interests or expectations. Accordingly, the source of value is found in the interests of individual persons.

Thus far the relationship of expectation to interest has been barely adumbrated. This topic will be covered more extensively in the section that follows. There is another matter worth introducing at this time.

Is it more proper to say that Perry derived the meaning of value by inference from behavior, or that Perry defined value in terms of behavior? Or, do these mean the same thing? The issue is centered on the distinction between deriving a meaning and defining. The former may be viewed as suggesting no more than the latter. In this sense it refers to the process of arriving at a definition. However, it may be taken in another much stronger sense as establishing a fact beyond question. The difference lies in the distinction between *viewing* 'value as any object of any interest' for conceptual purposes and asserting that 'value *is* any object of any interest.'

While he could infer interests and categorize them as positive and negative on the basis of his behavioristic approach, no amount of analysis of the term interest could establish it unequivocably as the source of value. In identifying 'positive interest' with 'good,' and 'negative interest' with 'bad,' Perry was making synthetic statements. There is no fault in this. All theories must rest ultimately on basic assumptions. However, these basic assumptions cannot themselves be derived from the theory without circularity no matter how the theory is manipulated or developed.

The significance of this issue will become more apparent as the discussion of the theory progresses. It has been introduced here in order to clarify just what had been accomplished in Perry's theory up to this point in the exposition. It is now time to return to the consideration of 'expectation.' In so doing the focus of attention is shifted from the concept of 'interest' to that of 'object.'

2. *Objects presented to interests—Perry's realism.*—One cannot be simply for or against, but must be for or against something. He must have an interest in some object. If the distinction between judging and valuing were to be maintained, interest could not be taken as a cognitive relationship with its object. An intermediary was required to link interests and objects. This was the function of the "mediating cognition." [26]

Perry insisted that "both interest and its mediating cognition are functions of the behaving organism." [27] The individual person must construe his object. It seems that interest depends, at least in part, upon cognition. Whatever the furniture of the world might be, the individual person can only be interested in it as he sees it, or as he judges it to be. Interest and therefore value depends upon the expectations of the individual concerning the nature of things. But in distinguishing interests and cognition had Perry solved the problem of vicious relativism? Was value established by any interest based on judgment or belief, or only by interest based on true judgment or belief? Did Perry establish a safe passage between relativistic and authoritarian views of truth concerning value or did he try to come down firmly on both sides of the fence, impaling himself on a fencepost in the process? On the surface the issue seems confused. Consider the following:

> No one can know the object of the agent's interest better than he does himself, for the object of the agent's interest is *what he judges,* whether he judges truly or falsely.
>
> [Furthermore,] if the agent does not know the object of his interest, no one does.[28]

Here, indeed, value seems to depend upon introspectionism. Perry stated that "As all judgment is liable to error, so all interest is . . . liable to failure or disappointment." [29] The more realistic the judgments involved, then the greater the chances of satisfying an interest. But suppose that someone's enjoyment of a painting is colored by the erroneous belief that Titian painted it. Does this mean that he really should enjoy the painting less than he does, or that he should not enjoy the painting? To prove to him that Titian did not paint it does not change the painting in any way, but it may change his attitude toward it. The painting itself is real; it is part of the furniture of the world. If his attitude towards it does change, was the painting the object of this agent's interest? He was interested in it *as a painting by Titian.* The correction of the error here seems to lead to a change in objects; he no longer views the painting as a Titian but as a non-Titian. But, what happens to the original interest? If the object is 'the painting as a Titian' and this object ceases to exist, then so too must the original interest cease to exist. On the basis of this example the only interest, and therefore value, that could survive such a test would be one based on true belief.

But was 'the painting as a Titian' the object of the agent's interest? 'The painting as a Titian' does not cease to exist; it *never* existed. In the above example it would have been more proper to say that the agent was interested in 'what he took to be a painting by Titian.' This was the course that Perry advocated. What was taken to be a painting by Titian? The very painting in question. On Perry's view, the interest in this case was an interest in the painting. The judgment had been in error; the object remained the same.[30]

The change in attitude then, was to stem from a change in judgment or belief. According to Perry there could be no interest in an object without the "interest-judgment," [31] the mediating cognition that presents the object to the interest. Perhaps Perry's discussion of the role of cognition in such terms as 'mediating' and 'presenting' suggests that cognition was to play a more aseptic role than was intended. His position may be clarified in reformulation.

What did Perry mean by "any object has value in so far as interest is taken in it"? He seems to have meant two things: first, that any real thing has value by virtue of being an object of interest, and second, that any real thing has value in accordance with the realism of the interest-judgment that colors the individual's conception of the object. The first is an assertion of the relativism of value with respect to interest; the second with respect to interest and realism of judgment. He avoided the pitfalls of Dewey's conception of truth which seemed to make judgment self-confirming, and the pitfalls of a dogmatic assertion that value had to be based on true judgment. The individual's judgment is to be tested by conformity to fact and not to whether he should continue to so judge in the future. At the same time the individual is to recognize that his knowledge is not absolute and while it requires constant retesting against reality it does participate in the process of value creation in the present. Perry advanced an ideal, the ideal of realism, at the same time that he failed to resolve the problem of value based on both the relativism of interest and the relativism of cognition. For, if value is to exist in the here and now, and not be withheld for the golden day in which all men have perfect knowledge or command of absolute truth, then value depends upon interest *and* the fallibility or reliability of judgment, or else it can make no sense to talk about testing values.

Perry *wanted* to talk about testing values.[32] He wanted to be able to compare values and to derive a conception of 'good,' 'better' and 'best' that would not be morally objectionable. This was the intent of his conception of harmonious integration of interests—first at the individual level and then among individuals. This conception represented Perry's solution to his problem, as outlined above, by the institution of a one step regress. The difficulty inherent in the solution is that of avoiding an infinite regress.

C. *Harmonious Integration of Interests—the Individual*

Perry stated that "the practical problem of everyday life is not to find goods. . . . The difficulty is to choose among goods, and to define principles by which such choice is justified." [33] An individual person has many interests and therefore many goods. The interests of any given individual may be compatible or incompatible. Incompatible interests may be viewed as rivals competing for the employment of "the same nerves, muscles, or energy" [34] of individuals at the same time. Activity in pursuit of the satisfaction of one cannot proceed simultaneously with activity in pursuit of the satisfaction of the other. Johnny can't play baseball and play the piano at the same time. Compatible interests do not compete. They may even reinforce one another. Johnny can play baseball and enjoy the company of his friends at the same time. Playing baseball may be the best way for him to insure his enjoyment of his friends' company and in turn the latter may enhance his enjoyment in playing baseball.

There is another sort of rivalry of interests according to Perry. Interests may be "contradictory." An individual may have "positive or negative interests in the same object . . . [and these] . . . cannot both be fulfilled." [35] Now, in this distinction Perry's assertion of the realism of the object was important. Thus, say Johnny has mixed feelings about becoming a fine pianist. Perry chose not to interpret these feelings as interests in different objects. But why not say that for Johnny becoming a fine pianist means attaining a power of mastery over a particular musical medium on the one hand and a life of constant toil and practice on the other? He has a positive interest in the former and a negative interest in the latter.

To some this might be morally objectionable. Practicing would be defined as bad and yet would be required as a necessary means to the good in this case. The resolution of this difficulty would be fairly simple if the negative interest in practicing were taken as a positive interest in not practicing. 'Not practicing' seems to be no more peculiar an object of interest than 'peace.' If behavior preventing the occurrence of war could serve as evidence that peace is the object of interest, then certainly behavior preventing the occurrence of practice would be evidence that not practicing is the object of interest. Despite the absence of a proper euphemism for not practicing, it would be an object of positive interest for Johnny.

However, Perry would not allow this interchange of the signs of interest and object. A positive interest in x was not the same thing as a negative interest in non-x.[36] Behavior preventing the occurrence of war was indicative of negative interest in war and not in itself positive interest in peace. Interests were not to be taken as mere logical categories, but rather as entities whose characters were to be inferred from behavior. If the individual acted to avoid some thing or some state of affairs then he had a negative interest in that object by definition. Now, 'not practicing' the piano is not a thing, nor is it an activity. Why does an object of interest have to be a thing or activity? Because things or activities exist or occur in the real world and Perry wanted his theory to be consistent with his realism. Still what difference does it make logically whether one infers from Johnny's behavior that he has an attitude of disfavor toward practicing piano or an attitude of favor toward not practicing piano. Both mean the same thing: Johnny would rather do other things than practice piano; Johnny would rather not forego doing other things than practice piano. He dislikes practicing the piano to the extent that he would rather do other things.

One might have taken a different track. Johnny might have been left with his negative interest in practicing piano. His positive interest in attaining a power of mastery over a musical medium might have been altered. Thus the latter might be viewed as a negative interest in not attaining such a power of mastery. Then contradiction could be viewed as a conflict involving a choice between the lesser of two evils. As a choice between goods or as a choice between evils, conflict becomes a problem of compatibility of interests. The notion of contradiction as Perry used it required, in effect, the assertion of the existence of positive and negative interests as entities in order to avoid their inter-translatability as logical categories. This is one way to avoid a controversy over whether 'less good' means 'worse' or 'less bad' means 'better.' And, if he were to advance a positive conception of the highest good, he needed some way of 'really' distinguishing good and evil. The way to the highest good was to be found in Perry's notion of the harmonious integration of interest. "*Harmony*, taken as the opposite of conflict . . . means non-contradiction and compatibility." [37] As Perry put it, "the central problem of integration is to achieve *harmony* in place of *conflict*." [38] The key terms in this last statement are 'problem' and 'achieve.' For, integration of interests was not something that just happened; it was to be viewed as a purposeful activity which could be pursued more or less intelligently. The individual was to take account of his interests and to organize them in such a way as to maximize his chances of securing the most good.

There were three questions that Perry had to answer in proposing harmonious integration as the solution to the problem of value. By what criteria are interests to be assigned their places in the organization? How was the individual to proceed in taking account of his interests? What sort of interest was it that conferred value on the organization of interests? Each of these questions will be considered in turn in the subsections that follow.

1. *Criteria for integration.*—The distinction must be made between taking account of interests and taking interests to account. They both require standards or criteria. The first requires standards for the ranking and comparing of interests in order to provide an organized view of one's interests and where they stand in relation to one another. The second requires criteria for determining where they ought to stand in relation to one another. One who would integrate his interests intelligently needs the data of the first sort of accounting in

order to proceed with the second, which is the business of integration.

This fairly simple statement about the requirements for criteria represents a refinement of perhaps the most confused and confusing aspect of Perry's theory. The chief difficulty arose from his determination to develop a conception of 'the good' from a description of good. He wanted an overlap in the two types of criteria so that interests could be ranked and weighted at once. As Perry saw the problem, not only did man have many goods, but he had many standards for ordering his goods. Somehow these standards had to be compared. At least this was his position in his earlier work, *The General Theory of Value*.[39] In the more recent publication, *The Realms of Value* his solution to the problem of comparing standards was to advance one criterion which evaded the problem. In the *Realms of Value* Perry listed the following standards:

> Preference, intensity, strength, duration, number, enlightenment, and inclusiveness of interest are all legitimate, and more or less explicitly recognized, modes of comparison. Intensity and preference provide comparison between different objects of the same interest; strength provides comparison between the interests of the same subject; number, duration, and enlightenment provide comparison *in these respects* between any interests of any subjects; and inclusion, or the whole-part relation, provides comparison between any interests in all respects.[40]

These standards may be further identified as follows: in taking account of his interest the individual might determine whether his interest in x is fairly intense or only lukewarm, whether he prefers x to y, whether the strength of his interest in x is such that it tends to be prepotent or inhibiting with regard to other interests time and time again, whether his interest in y can be maintained as long at one sitting as his interest in x, whether he has several interests in x and fewer in y, whether his interest in x does not have the same quality as it might have with more knowledge and training, and whether his interest in x also includes an interest in z. The "objects of greater interest, however measured," were, according to Perry, "better than the objects of lesser." There could be "no objection to the admission of all these standards provided they are [sic] not confused with one another."[41] The trouble was that they could be easily confused with one another and, moreover, they made the theory more confusing.

Consider, for example, the standards of intensity, preference, and strength. Suppose that wine and water were taken as the objects of the same interest.[42] How is a choice to be made between them? Without different interests in them they cannot have different values, unless there is something about these objects that affects the same interest differently. Do objects have peculiar qualities for reflecting values in different ways? His attack on G. E. Moore precluded his taking this sort of position.

Well, then, suppose wine and water are taken as subcategories of the object 'something to drink' and interest in wine and interest in water as subcategories of interest in 'something to drink.' What sort of object is 'something to drink'? It is a generalization, an abstraction from specific objects. An intense interest in 'something to drink' will not help one to decide between wine and water, but it might make a difference in deciding between pursuing these objects and pursuing the objects of other types of interest. If, however, one attempts to decide between wine and water on the basis of the intensities of the respective interests in them, then what happens to the distinction between intensity and preference?

If intensity is taken to be a quality of interest in an object at a specific time and preference the quality of the relationship between certain interests in objects over time, the distinction might be maintained. One usually prefers wine but this time he would rather have a drink of water. Does this mean that at this time the intensity of his interest in water is greater than that of his interest in wine, or that it is enough to overcome his preference for wine? Is his preference for wine distinguishable from the strength of his interest in wine? One could say that of all things he might drink, while he prefers some things to others, he will almost always drink wine. Common language would permit him to say that he has an intense interest in wine, a strong interest in wine, or a great preference for wine.

In stipulating meanings for 'intensity,' 'preference' and 'strength' Perry denied this sort of translatability. There is nothing reprehensible about such stipulation so long as it is recognized as stipulation. The crucial consideration is whether it raises confusion or conduces to clarity. In speaking of 'intensity' and 'preference' as standards for comparing objects of the same interests and of 'strength' for comparing interests, Perry did not enhance the clarity of his theory; he made it more confusing. The comparison of value consistent with Perry's theory must be more than a comparision of interests or objects; it must be a comparision of interests *in* objects.

In the *General Theory of Value* the distinction between standards were more important than in the *Realms of Value*. In the earlier publication 'good,' 'better' and 'best' were defined in their most significant terms by the principles of intensity, preference, and inclusiveness. Integration was to proceed in accordance with an order of applicability of these principles.[43] It is difficult to tell whether Perry recognized the confusions in his criteria. In the later publication none of the standards were dropped, but 'good,' 'better' and 'best' were defined in terms of any of the standards. The order of applicability was dropped and the principle of inclusiveness became *the* criterion for integration. Attention is focussed on the more recent position on the assumption that it was Perry's most considered or, perhaps, more properly, his reconsidered view:

> There is an inveterate tendency to assume that an interest that is superior in one respect is superior in all respects. There is only one respect of which this can be said, namely, inclusiveness. If one interest includes another interest it possesses and exceeds all the magnitudes which the included interest possesses. A whole must be more than its parts—otherwise the term 'partial' would lose its meaning. The standard of inclusion escapes the problem of commensurability by not raising it. To say that a total interest is greater than any of its partial interests *whatever their magnitudes* escapes the necessity of comparing these magnitudes among themselves.

> Here again it is necessary to resist the temptation to claim too much. The standard of inclusiveness does not annul or supersede other standards, but omits them without prejudice. It defines the framework within which life may rise through other rankings of inferiority and superiority.[44]

When may one interest be said to include another? Perry used as an example a man's interest in water. It included his interest in water for bathing and water for drinking.[45] In choosing between wine and water, he chooses water because it serves more interests; it is more inclusive. Now, is it proper to speak of water as the object of two interests or are water for bathing' and 'water for drinking' to be taken as two separate objects? In ordinary terms one may be interested in water for several reasons and may speak of his interest in water as a general reference for these reasons. Interest in water then means interest in water for a, interest in water for b, interest in water for c, etc. Interest in water is manifested by endeavor to obtain or maintain the supply of water necessary for the satisfaction of any or all of these interests. The greater the interest in water, i.e. the more inclusive the interest in water, the greater the value of water. Thus far this says no more than 'the four interests in wa, wb, wc, and wd together confer more value on w than interests in wa, wb and wc.'

The choice, however, is between water and wine. The value of water, whatever it is, must be compared with the value of wine. To say in this case that interest in water is more inclusive than interest in wine is to say only that there are more interests in water than in wine. In effect this would be to make number the major criterion of value. Number was involved in the criterion of inclusiveness as indicated above, but it operated only in a whole-part relationship of interests. If the choice between wine and water is to be decided by the principle of inclusiveness, then if water is chosen it would seem that interest in wine must somehow be taken as part of interest in water. This would be stretching things a bit far.

Interest in an even more general object is required. Interest in liquids includes interest in liquids for drinking, interest in liquids for cooking, interest in liquids for maintaining bodily cleanliness, interests in liquids for watering crops and/or livestock, etc. Suppose the choice is between wine and no water on the one hand and water and no wine on the other. Let l symbolize liquid; y, wine; w, water; and a, b, c, d, . . . n all the ways in which a given individual is concerned with liquids. la, lb, lc, ld, . . . ln are liquids for drinking, liquids for bathing, etc. Interest in la, lb, lc, ld, . . . $ln =$ interest in (wa or ya), wb, wc, wd, . . . wn. A choice for y is a choice for one part of the series, la, to the exclusion of lb . . . ln. A choice for w is a choice for the whole series $la \ldots ln$. Interest in w therefore confers greater value than interest in y by the principle of inclusion.

The application of the principle of inclusion moves from an analysis of an interest in an object into its component interests in objects to the generation of interests in objects which can include other interests in objects. In the first case the meaning of an interest in an object is made more explicit by breaking things down into components. In the second case interests in objects are given meaning by collecting them under a more general heading. In the first case the structure of interests in objects is examined for relationships; in the second, interests in objects are restructured to provide relationships. In the first case one is taking account of his interests to see how his values are arranged; in the second, he is taking his interests to account, to see how his values ought to be arranged or integrated.

In the *General Theory of Value* Perry stated that the principle of "inclusiveness makes possible the comparison of the objects of one interest with the objects of another without the introduction of a third interest." [46] Where the whole-part relation between specific interests in objects is already recognized by the interested individual, this may be true. However, in every case where an interest in an object has to be formulated to include interests in objects it would seem that another interest has been introduced. To say that this is not really a new interest because it includes the others is to say in the end that each person has one interest that includes all the others. This is what Perry did say and what he meant by total interest. This position will become clearer as it is developed more fully in the discussion of the process of rational reflection.

2. *The process of rational reflection.*—The application of the principle of inclusiveness involved the process of rational reflection. Just as the former could be taken in two different senses, the latter had two senses corresponding to those, respectively. In taking stock of one's values, one may proceed more or less rationally. One may endeavor to take all of his interests into account, or he may try to avoid facing the fact that he has certain interests. He may not want to admit that there is a relationship between two of his interests. In this sense his judgment concerning the structure of his values may be more or less objective, more or less colored by particular interests, more or less coldly rational.

The process of rational reflection in the second sense of the application of the principle of inclusiveness, depends upon the rationality of the application of the first sense. Restructuring depends upon an adequate grasp of the original structure. But, it goes beyond this. Perry put the matter as follows:

> Rationalization is not a mere stating of his reasons by the agent. It is a finding of new reasons, or the introduction of new mediating judgments. These have the effects of linking interests in new ways, or of introducing integration where it did not exist before. . . . They bring interests into new relations through common objects, or through making one the object of another. Rationalization is the introduction of such acts of mediation for the sake of the integration which it effects. Its purpose is to attract to any interest or to its object, the favor and support of other interests. It may therefore be termed 'justification' or 'apologetic reasoning.'

> The result of rationalization is often to create a new end which is distinguished by its integrative character,

or by the fact that it is confluent with many interests, drawing them together, embodying them, satisfying them, and engaging them jointly.[47]

Such rationalization is not to be dismissed summarily "either as gratuitous, or as self-deceptive and mendacious." [48] This is not a matter of fooling one's self or taking a sour grapes attitude toward an object that is given less value after reflection than it was given before. The element of the non-rational is recognized in that interests themselves are ultimately grounded in propensities, dispositions, likes and dislikes. At the same time Perry insisted that it is "pertinent to apply the terms 'true' and 'false' to an interest. . . . " He contended that "every interested act has a reason, for every interested act has at least one mediating judgment. . . . " As he put it, "No interested act is understood until . . . it has been made to *seem* reasonable in terms of those expectations with which it was associated in the agent." [49]

Perry was on rather slippery ground here. It may be granted that every interested act has a reason and, if performed, this reason must have seemed a good reason to the agent. Here, however, the issue over testing a value is raised. To call an interest true or false is to suggest that the value of an interest depends upon the truth or falsity of the mediating cognition. Rationalization or rational reflection proceeds by considering the existing reasons for following interests and then judging the merits of interests in the light of possible reasons for following them. The integration of interest on the principle of inclusiveness by the process of rational reflection appears to make judgment of interests the source of value while paying lip service to interest.

Perry's denial of this allegation was, in effect, to view rational reflection as the set of mediating cognitions for a superior interest. This was where his conception of total interest came in. Rational reflection viewed as integration was to mediate the individual's interest in his own greatest good. This introduces the topic of the inclusive self-interest.

3. *The inclusive self-interest.*—At the heart of Perry's concept of harmonious integration of interest lies the notion of the inclusive self-interest. It represents the positive interest of the individual in his interests. It is the interest of the individual in the success of his interests. It is self-interest in the extreme. It defines the person and it defines morality.

Perry stated that a "man is a person insofar as there is a central clearing-house where his interests . . . take account of one another, and are allowed to proceed only when the demands of other interests are consulted and wholly or partially met." [50] Rational reflection by the principles of inclusiveness was the essence of personality on this view. Personal integrity, the identity of a person as a person, was defined as the individual's integration of his interests. Moral integrity seems to have been identified with personal integrity. Consider the following:

Morality is the solution of the problem created by conflict—conflict among the interests of the same or of different persons. The solution of the personal problem lies in the substitution for a condition of warring and mutually destructive impulses a condition in which each impulse being assigned a limited place, may be innocent and contributory. For the weakness of inner discord it substitutes the strength of a unified life in which several interests of an individual make common cause together. [51]

From this definition of morality as harmonious integration of interests, Perry developed his conception of the moral interest.

When interests are thus organized there emerges an interest of the totality, or moral interest, whose superiority lies in its being greater than any of its parts— greater by the principle of inclusiveness. It is authorized to speak for all of the component interests when its voice is their joint voice. The height of any claim in the moral scale is proportional to the breadth of its representation. What suits all of a person's interests is exalted above what merely suits a fraction; what suits everybody is exalted above what suits somebody.[52]

Leaving aside for the moment "what suits everybody" this is what is meant by self-interest in the extreme. It is a self-interest that cannot tolerate the pursuit of the object of one interest at the expense of all others. It does omit standards without prejudice, but it does not omit interests without prejudice; it does not steer a safe course between the hazards of vicious relativism and absolutism; it does interpose a third interest in the choice between interests; it evades all of these problems and solves none of them.

Consider the case of an individual with a strong interest in alcohol. In his lucid moments he sits down and reflects quite rationally on all his interests. He considers every one of them and organizes them. He decides that his interest in alcohol is his most important interest and judges each interest in terms of its bearing on this. Interest in alcohol thus includes all his other interests. It is his most inclusive interest. He satisfies all other interests only to the extent that he must in order to attain the object of his interest in alcohol. Each impulse has been assigned its limited place. There is no weakness of inner discord; there is the strength of a unified life. Does 'What suits all of a person's interests' mean any more than this? Substitute, in the above example, a strong interest in murdering people. Are these clear cases of moral integrity?

The standard of strength has been omitted without prejudice; it has been ignored. In being ignored it colors the individual's view of every one of his interests. He cannot view them without prejudice and if he omits any of them as not conducing to his strong interest he omits them with prejudice. His interests in his objects are what they seem to be to him. Let his integration of these interests be a bit less 'rational' than in the example above. He may still be quite satisfied with his integration. So long as he doesn't know any better, he is quite happy and he may not care to know any better. Is moral integrity reserved only for the perfectly rational? If so, then value for the individual depends ultimately upon perfect reason, and this is absolutism. If not, then ultimate value for the individual may be grounded in judgment colored by interest and this leads to vicious relativism. Finally, what sense can be made of Perry's contention that the total interest speaks for all interests? What manner of abstraction is this interest in all of one's interests?

If a man is interested in x he is interested in x. Where does an interest in his interest in x come from? If he is interested in x, y and z, he wants to satisfy his interests in x, y and z or else he would not really be interested in them. Does an interest in all of his interests differ somehow from the total of these interests? If it does not, then how can choices be made among them? Choices have to be made, for all of them cannot be satisfied; some of them conflict. Interest in all of one's interests, then, must mean interest in the attainment of the maximum good for the individual. But, then, this is an interest in satisfying enough of the right interests for the attainment of the maximum good. In deciding what interests should be satisfied, all interests may be considered but it seems odd to say that those which are rejected or are given a very limited chance at satisfaction are rejected or limited in their own interests. In practical terms this sort of consideration may be the best way to maximize the attainment of objects of interest. However, interest in maximizing the attainment of the objects of interest cannot be the same thing as the totality of interest, because some interests must be sacrificed in its behalf. Consequently, a third interest has been introduced for the purpose of comparing and ordering other interests.

This opens the door to two sorts of difficulties. On the one hand the concept of interest becomes confused; on the other, value may become mired in an infinite regress. A positive interest in an object is itself a disposition in favor of the attainment of its object and this object is good. If positive interest in this object must await consideration in the interest of maximizing the attainment of the objects of interest, then this superior interest defines the good of all objects of interest. Now what is the source of value, any interest or only this superior interest? This superior interest is dependent upon all of the interests in objects as the goods to be organized. Each of these interests is at the same time dependent upon the superior interest for the determination of its worthiness to be satisfied and thus the value of each interest is derived from this superior interest. The object of any positive interest is good, but is it good enough? The notion of 'good enough,' like the notion of 'true interest,' maintains interest as the source of value, but in effect may make Perry's theory of value indistinguishable in operation from the operation of value-judgment in Perry's conception of Dewey's theory.

What sort of interest is this superior interest? It is a positive interest in maximizing the satisfaction of positive interests. What makes a positive interest worth being included? Could it be a positive interest in this interest's being satisfied? Good, then, would be positive interest in the satisfaction of positive interest. However, as has already been indicated, all interests cannot be satisfied. Does this mean that good is only the object of any positive interest which is also itself the object of positive interest? If so, then, this last positive interest must either be treated as any positive interest and therefore the position leads to an infinite regress, or else some reason must be given for treating it as a special kind of positive interest which stops the regression. To call it the moral interest and thus the source of moral good as opposed to any old good[53] does not help. For, since Perry equated being a person with integrating interests, either all persons are *ipso facto* moral, or all non-moral"?" are non-persons. Moreover, where does this moral interest come from? Does it stem from nature as other interests are supposed to stem? It has already been referred to as a superior interest, but is it the most superior interest? For the answers to these questions, the discussion must turn from the examination of good for the person to the examination of good for people.

D. *Harmonious Integration of Interests—Among Individuals*

Interests of several individuals often conflict. The murderer, for example, in following his interest, however inclusive it might be for him, excludes all the interests of his victim. There is no group mind to integrate these conflicting interests: "Excluding fictitious persons, legal persons, and every metaphysical or figurative use of the term, the only real person is that being which is capable of reflecting, choosing, relating means to ends, making decisions, and subordinating particular interests to an overruling purpose." [54] The problem of harmonious integration of interest among individuals is to translate overruling purpose from inclusive self-interest to some sort of inclusive social interest without presuming a thinking social entity as the agent. The examination of the translation as it developed, parallels that of the development of the original.

1. *Criteria broadened.*—At bottom, the issue for Perry's theory of value was to account for the commensurability of interests on the inter-individual level. He stated:

> When men's values conflict, each endeavors to prove that his is superior. The problem of the critique and grading of value is properly emphasized in that important branch of theory of value which deals with morality; for morality is not only a domain of value but a level or plane of value, claiming preeminence over other value.[55]

Once again the distinction must be made between taking account of values and taking values to account—between recognizing values and comparing them. In listing the modes of comparison, Perry limited them according to the contexts of their applicability. If these limitations were questionable at the level of individual integration, they are even more questionable at the level of social integration. Thus, if the objects involved are taken to be the same for all the individuals concerned, it does make sense to say that Jones has a more intense interest in x than Smith, or that Jones prefers x to y more than Smith does. The difficulty of distinguishing intensity, preference and strength is not eliminated. What's more one must be careful not to confuse any of the criteria with the criterion of number. If ninety members of a group of one hundred people have positive interests in x, one cannot say that the group has a strong interest in x. The interests of the individual members in x may run from very mild interest to very strong. Finally, there is still the problem of the commensurability of criteria. Jones' interest in x is more enlightened than Smith's, but Smith's is more intense. If they can be said to have an interest in the same x, which interest confers more value on x?

The principle of inclusiveness, as before, was to omit all other criteria without prejudice. Suppose Jones' interest in x is more inclusive for him than Smith's interest in x. Does this mean that Jones has a better claim to the possession of x than Smith? Comparison by the principle of inclusiveness was comparison of a part with its whole. In the case at hand x is worth more to Jones than to Smith on the basis of their respective part-whole comparisons. To decide who should have x by the principles of inclusion, there must be a whole which includes both Jones' and Smith's interests in x.

Now it may be prudent for each of them to consider the interest of the other before pursuing his claim. Smith may be the type who is willing to fight at the drop of a hat. Jones may be smaller and weaker than Smith, and his interest in x may have to be limited by a more inclusive concern for his own well-being. However, this does not say anything to the relative merits of their individual claims on x, unless one takes the position that might makes right and the devil take the hindmost. Perry would not take this position.

In this example Jones is not taking Smith's interest in x as Smith's interest in x; he is taking it as a sign for a part of his own well-being. What is required is a whole that can include Jones' and Smith's interests in x, as they are for Jones and Smith. Perry stated that "what suits everybody is exalted above what suits somebody." [56] The most inclusive whole, then, is an interest in suiting everybody.

Everyone can't be suited in everything. Suppose there is only one x, that an interest in x can be satisfied only by the consumption of x, and that Jones and Smith are everybody. They cannot both satisfy their interests in x. Does more good result for everybody if Jones gets x or if Smith gets x? If they each have an interest in the interests of everybody, then

Jones' self-interest is on a par with Smith's self-interest for each of them. Because Jones' interest in x is more inclusive than Smith's, more value for everybody would result from the satisfaction of Jones' interest in x.

At the interindividual level the principal of inclusiveness requires the creation of an interest in an object at a higher level of generality than inclusive self-interest. Each individual is to take account of his interests and take them to account or restructure them by the principle of inclusiveness. Then he is to take account of the value structures of himself and others as they stand and take these to account, restructure, or integrate them by the principle of inclusiveness.[57]

Integration at the individual level involved the introduction of an interest in maximizing the satisfaction of one's own interests. Now it seems that yet another interest must be introduced, an interest in maximizing the satisfaction of everyone's self-interest. Why should anyone have such an interest? Should everyone have such an interest? Perry's answers to these questions may be considered more closely as his conception of the role of rational reflection is developed and examined.

2. *The role of rational reflection.*—The success of harmonious integration among individuals depends in part upon the adequacy and accuracy of each individual's consideration of the self-interests of all concerned. "There are degrees of reflection. It may be comparatively hasty, shallow, impulsive, irrational, or it may be comparatively deliberate, deep, wholehearted, rational." [58] If Jones is to take account of Smith's self-interest he must try to see it as Smith sees it. Presuming that Smith is a rational adult, his self-interest is what he takes it to be, and not what Jones may think it ought to be. The more adequate Smith's consideration of his interests the better he is able to integrate his interests to maximize his good. The

more adequate each person's picture of his own self-interest as well as the self-interests of others, the better may these be integrated to maximize good for all. The picture of all self-interests depends for its clarity and freedom from distortion upon the openness and frankness of communication and discussion.

Honest and free discussion was the extension of rational reflection to the inter-individual level. As such it was more than the means for taking account of interests; it also served as the method for integrating interests. Rational reflection by the individual and free communication among individuals were taken as different levels of the method of reflective agreement. Perry put this as follows:

> Morality is an integration of interests, in which they are rendered harmonious without losing their identity. The procedure by which this is effected is the method of *reflective agreement,* appearing in the personal will, and in the social will. . . .

> The similarity between the personal and social forms of the moral will must not be allowed to obscure their profound difference. It is true that as the personal will emerges from reflection so the social will emerges from communication and discussion. In both cases the emergent will represents a totality of interests, and achieves by organization a substitution of harmony for conflict. The difference lies in the fact that whereas the personal will is composed of sub-personal interests, the social will is composed of persons.[59]

Now, just as personal integration proceeded by the evaluation of reason or reasons involved in interest-judgment, interpersonal integration was to proceed through reflective agreement on reasons. Each agent was to advance reasons in support of his claims and listen to the reasons of others in support of their claims. Agreement was to be reached on the basis of reflection on all these reasons, without bias toward one's own or anyone else's. Through discussion people were to come to agreement on the most reasonable integration of personal interests. The more reasonable all the individuals concerned, the more reasonable the agreement, the more harmonious the integration of interests.

Why should anyone communicate honestly and freely with others? His self-interest may be served best if everyone else did so and he did not. He could better maximize his self-interest at their expense. Or, why shouldn't the most enlightened and the most rational engage in open and frank discussion with all others in order that he might integrate all interests for the good of all? The first question asks why anyone should care about maximizing any good other than his own. The second question asks to what extent everyone must participate actively in the discussions involved in harmonious integration.

Perry's answer to the first question was, in effect, an assertion that the highest good for anybody is his highest good consistent with the highest good for everybody. If everybody selfishly tried to maximize personal good, the condition of man would be one of constant war with all men. Agreement and consideration of interests of others would occur for basically selfish reasons. Cunning, power, and aggressiveness would define the highest good. The best that any individual should have would be the best that he could get for himself. Is this morally objectionable? It is on Perry's definition of morality. But this definition of morality is precisely what is at issue here. In stating that "there can be no moral will on the social level except as composed of several personal wills which are peculiarly modified and interrelated," [60] Perry asserted that the socially moral person could not be selfish. The issue was to be resolved by seeing to it that no one was selfish.

Suppose an ideal situation in which there are no selfish people. Should the wisest decide on the best integration of personal interests? Everyone would sit down with 'big brother' and 'big brother' would tell them what to do. As Perry saw things, this would not do even in this ideal situation. If no one can know the interest of any given individual as well as that individual, the best assurance that the interests of all individuals are adequately represented in harmonious integration would be for all individuals to participate actively in the construction of the integration. No matter how wise 'big brother' might be and no matter how open and free communication might be, 'big brother' can never presume to know the inclusive self-interests of all individuals as well as they do themselves.

The self-interest of the individual need not be static or absolutely stable. In the process of communication and discussion, it does not remain unaffected. This is what Perry meant by personal will emerging from reflection and social will emerging from discussion. The social will is a will of persons. In the process of reaching agreement personal will is structured and restructured by the reflecting individual. He does not merely tell others of his personal interest; he develops his personal interest along with others through communication and discussion for the purpose of agreement.[61] Each person must have an interest in maximizing good for all as evidenced by his willing participation with other individuals in the harmonious integration of interests. What sort of an interest in what sort of object is this?

3. *The inclusive benevolent interest.*—Benevolent interest on the part of each individual was to color inclusive self-interest in such a way as to make harmonious integration on the interpersonal level an intra-personal good. Perry explained what he meant by benevolence: "The term 'benevolence' had best be reserved for positive, independent interest in the fulfillment of another's interest . . . benevolence is to seek to further it." [62] Benevolence was to operate in the following manner:

> Taking your desires and aversions, your hopes and fears, your pleasures and pains, in short, the interests by which you are actually moved, I act as though these interests were my own. Though I cannot, strictly speaking, *feel* your interests, I can acknowledge them, wish them well, and allow for them in addition to the interests which are already embraced within me.[63]

It is clear in this passage that benevolence did not mean that the interests of others were to supplant one's own. One was to allow for them in addition to one's own and not above one's own. Perry stated that, "benevolence is no more essential to the personal will than is hunger or an interest in collecting postage stamps. The social will, on the other hand, must be benevolent. Thus the social will is subjected to a double requirement, personality *and* benevolence." [64] The social will *must* be benevolent in the sense that this was part of Perry's definition of social will. It had to be personal because, according to Perry, there was no will except of persons.

Just as personal will was inclusive self-interest, social will was inclusive benevolent interest. Perry asserted that "when there is a social will among several persons the conduct which it prescribes will coincide with that which is prescribed by the personal will of each, but that will be only because benevolence has already been introduced into the personal will." [65] Perry went on to assert the following:

> The principal of moral organization requires that the good of the whole shall take precedence of the several goods of the members, when and only when it embraces them and provides for them. There is only one way in which this can be achieved, namely by a universal social will arrived at by reflective social agreement. Such a will exists distributively in each human person; while at the same time it represents all personal wills because the harmony which each person has achieved for himself then embraces every other person.[66]

In effect, Perry was saying that 'social will exists among persons when the personal will of each of these persons is organized in the interest of all personal wills.' However, what did he mean by 'universal social will' and by his contention that the conduct prescribed by social will is the conduct prescribed by each participant in the social will? Is social will possible only when all people view things in precisely the same manner? People cannot view things in precisely the same manner.

Inclusive benevolent interest as interest in the self-interests of all individuals was an interest in maximizing good for all people by reflective social agreement. Insofar as each individual is interested in maximizing good for all, he is interested in reaching agreement on the optimum organization of the interests of all. By virtue of his interest and participation in agreement he wills the result of the process of agreement, whatever it should turn out to be.

This is not quite the same thing as prescribing what it turns out to be. An individual may say, 'For the sake of harmony I'll go along with the decision, but I personally don't believe that it is the right decision. I still think that a different course of action would be more conducive to the good of all.'

Now, Perry wanted to allow for this; indeed he insisted upon it.[67] The problem here is analogous to the problem raised by his conception of totality of interest at the individual level. Maximizing the satisfaction of interests required the limitation or the suppression of some interests in the process of integration by rational reflection. Interest in the totality of interests could only make sense as interest in maximizing the satisfaction of interests. But, interests of persons conflict. Interest in maximizing the satisfaction of personal interests requires the limitation or suppression of some personal interests. However, the notion of personal interest has undergone a peculiar change. Because personal interest is to be so colored by benevolence, conflict of personal interest has become conflict of personal social interest. The murderer must justify his interest as conducing to the maximization of all personal interests. He can not be interested in murder for the sense of well-being he derives from it; he must consider it in the light of the well-being of society. If interest and reflection require individual organisms, then in the society in pursuit of harmonious integration, the members can, in effect, only disagree about the optimum integration for maximizing the good of all. When, through discussion, individuals, agree on optimum integration, they are said to be of one mind. But are they, and about what?

This may be the best practical procedure for maximizing the attainment of the good for all. Each member may feel that a different integration would be better, but that this integration is better than no integration. They may be of one mind only in the belief that this is the best practical means to maximize the attainment of the good for all. They agree unanimously that they must come to an agreement. They need not agree unanimously that the agreement reached is the best. Some may speak against it, but benevolence requires that they must agree to order their behavior in accordance with it. There is nothing to prevent them from trying to convince others through further discussion that a new agreement would be better.

What is 'good' on this view? Good is any object of any interest. But interests must themselves be judged good in the light of maximizing personal interest. So, good is the object of positive interest in the object of positive interest. Now personal interest is itself to be evaluated on the basis of positive interest in all personal interests. So good is to be the object of positive interest in positive interest in positive interest. Perry based his theory on the contention that it is inherent in the nature of man to have interests and that these interests define good. Now it seems that value was to depend ultimately upon an interest that had to be implanted in man. Perry's theory of value was consistent with the nature of man in the sense that man could have such an interest and not in the sense that he did have such an interest.

This makes judgment the ultimate source of value. In the last analysis it is the judgment that value should be defined by the inclusive benevolent interest that is at issue. In effect, Perry's Theory of Value has value insofar as one judges that it has value. This is the topic of the general critique which now follows.

E. *The Egocentric Predicament and Perry's Theory of Value*

There is something peculiar about the quest for a theory of value that would not be morally objectionable. A general theory of value must define moral value. How then is the theory to be judged in the light of moral value without circularity? Perry wanted a theory which would provide one solution to two distinct problems, how to conceive recognition of the good in individual terms without falling into the abyss of vicious relativism, and how to construe obligation in individual terms without appeal to external authority. Perry's theory may be judged as to how well it met these conditions. However, in setting these conditions Perry begged the question of their justification. One may want to judge the theory on the basis of the worthiness of these conditions and this the theory cannot allow. The value of the conditions must be assumed in the theory. The truth of the basic assumptions of any theory cannot be proved by the theory, and in Perry's theory these were basic assumptions. However, people do pick and choose among theories, and some are discarded even though their internal logical structures might be flawless. How does one evaluate a theory which tells him how he should value it?

1. *The problem of knowing interests of others.*—The attempt has been made throughout this discussion to maintain the distinction between theorizing about things as they are and theorizing about things as they might become. Perhaps the most serious weakness in Perry's theory is his failure to maintain this sort of distinction. He did not refer to what value 'would become' as a result of agreement but he chose to speak of what value 'is' as a result of agreement. Theorizing about the way things might become can be viewed in two different lights; as an assertion that something can work in a specified manner or as an assertion that something ought, ideally, to work in particular ways.

In the examination of inclusive self-interest it was noted that unless perfect reason and knowledge were presumed, integration and thus value are not free from relativism. Again, at the level of harmonious integration among individuals agreement must be colored by relativism of judgment despite the benevolence of all the participants. No one can really know the interests of others, and as they engage in discussion for the sake of agreement, each person's conception of the optimum integration is affected by his own limitations of judgment. Clearly, Perry's theory of value could not actually work in a manner that would be free from vicious relativism as he defined it.

Nevertheless, it could also be viewed as an ideal, as a goal that can never be attained, but which does make a difference to practice. One can try his best not to let his interests color his judgment. He can insist upon the difference between value and judgment about value. He can take account of interests and take them to account as he insists that values are not created by judgment and that every interest has a claim to satisfaction. Judgment about interests and the world in which they act may be more or less true. The more realistic the agent is about his interests and about the world, the more realistic may be the integration of his interests for his maximum satisfaction. One can wallow in the practical limitations of the condition of man or he can attempt to make the best terms with them. The latter was the ideal that Perry proposed. It was the ideal of the relativism of value supported by the realism of knowledge. This raises another question.

2. *Is benevolence justified as a goal?*—A problem arises over the justification of this ideal. Joel Feinberg accused Perry of committing a sort of naturalistic fallacy.[68] Charles L. Stevenson accused Perry of having failed to maintain the distinction between description and decision.[69] Their charges focus upon the same point.

Perry's approach to the problem of the naturalistic fallacy was two-pronged. First, he asserted the analyzability of value in terms of human interests. He sought to distinguish value expressions in use from the theoretic reconstruction of their usage.[70] In essence, he proposed a theory of the way value expressions ought to be used if value was to be construed in terms of human interests. Still, one could invoke Moore's open question argument[71] against construing value in terms of human interests rather than, say, God's interests. However, (the second prong) one might prefer a naturalistic theory in opposition to its alternatives. And Perry did provide a definition of value broad enough to avoid dispute through the open question argument as to whether, for example, good was the object of pleasure or of desire; interest included both.

But Perry's theory still runs into difficulty with the introduction of the principle of inclusion as reflective agreement. In the principles of inclusive self-interest, and inclusive benevolent interest, Perry asserted that judgment and agreement defined 'better' and 'best.' As Stevenson noted "to describe how people make ethical decisions is not to make an ethical decision. Perry goes [sic] on to make an ethical decision of his own, saying that an object becomes better when, all else being equal, someone's attitudes to it become reinforced." [72] The reinforcement was to result from judgment in the interest of maximizing the satisfaction of self-interest and this in turn was to be colored by judgment in the interest of maximizing the satisfaction of all self-interests.

At the first level one may ask why the highest value for the individual is not defined by his strongest interest over time or his most intense interest at any time. To say that the individual would be better off by controlling such interests in his own interest is to beg the question. At the level of interpersonal inclusion, someone could ask, for example, why the highest value should not be defined by the most inclusive self-interest of the strongest individual. Again to assert that all would be better off by controlling such interest is to beg the question. There was nothing in Perry's *definition* of value that made morality at the individual or social level obligatory. Perry asserted additional definitions of *higher* value to insure obligation. He defined morality in specific ways as the higher and highest good and in so doing committed the naturalistic fallacy at these higher levels. In effect, Perry has said that while good is the object of any positive interest it ought to be the object of positive interest in interest in interest. For the individual who accepts Perry's definitions of morality, that is the definition of good. For the person who does not accept Perry's view of morality, good is the object of any interest.

Why should anyone accept Perry's definition of morality? Stevenson suggested the following reason:

> It is acknowledged that *if* Perry's persuasive definitions of "better" and "worse" are accepted, he has provided a standard of comparative values which has the advantage over many others in being intelligible, and applicable to concrete cases—not applicable in any simple or wholly rigorous way, of course, but at least in a way that may be roughly practicable. . . . His work . . . serves the purpose of making articulate an important type of ethical norm.[73]

As both Stevenson and Feinberg noted, Perry's theory of value appears to support certain democratic ideals.[74] Perry's problem of justifying the objective of inclusive benevolent interest may be viewed in two lights. On the one hand it was the problem of describing and justifying the ideal democratic society. On the other hand it was the problem of creating the ideal democratic society. The first was the subject of Perry's theory of society; the second, of his theory of education. Democracy required a theory of value and a theory of education which promoted and supported democracy. But does the inclusive benevolent interest justify democracy, or does democracy justify the indoctrination of the inclusive benevolent interest?

1. GTV, pp. 115–16; Perry's italics.

2. Ralph Barton Perry, "The Question of Moral Obligation," *International Journal of Ethics*, XXI, No. 3 (1911), 291; Perry's italics.

3. RV, pp. 127–30.

4. Ibid., pp. 123–26.

5. Ralph Barton Perry, *International Journal of Ethics*, XXI, No. 3, 292–93.

6. GTV, p. 30, and see G. E. Moore, *Principia Ethica* (paperback ed., London: Cambridge University Press, 1959), p. 10.

7. See, for example, John Dewey, *The Quest for Certainty: A Study of the Relation of Knowledge and Action* (Capricorn ed.; New York: G. Putnam Son's Co., 1960), pp. 260–61; Dewey's italics and quotes.

8. GTV, p. 123, note 17; Perry's italics.

9. Ralph Barton Perry, *Present Philosophical Tendencies: A Critical Survey of Naturalism, Idealism, Pragmatism, and Realism Together with a Synopsis of the Philosophy of William James* (New York: Longmans, Green & Co., 1912), p. 332; Perry's italics.

10. GTV, p. 139.

11. GTV, p. 116.

12. Ibid.

13. John Dewey, *Theory of Valuation*, International Encyclopedia of Unified Science, Foundations of the Unity of Science, II, No. 4, (Chicago: University of Chicago Press, 1939), 18–19.

14. GTV, p. 141.

15. Ibid., p. 115; Perry's italics.

16. Ibid., pp. 140–45.

17. Ibid., and see esp. pp. 270–71.

18. Ibid., chap. vi, sec. iii, esp. pp. 177–79.

19. Ibid., chap. vii passim, esp. sec. ii, p. 184 f.

20. Ibid., p. 230; Perry's italics.

21. Ibid., p. 235.

22. RV, p. 3; Perry's italics.

23. GTV, p. 235.

24. RV, p. 101; Perry's quotes and italics.

25. Ibid., pp. 76–78 and GTV, pp. 235–37.

26. RV, p. 35 f. and GTV, chap. xii.

27. GTV, p. 521.

28. Ibid., p. 360; Perry's italics.

29. Ibid., p. 346, see also pp. 611–15 for Perry's discussion of testing values.

30. Cf. ibid., pp. 360–61 and 611–15. See esp. p. 612.

31. Ibid., pp. 345–50.

32. Thus he stated "The object of true or enlightened interest is better than the object of false. . . . " RV, p. 84. See also p. 59 f.

33. RV, p. 50.

34. GTV, p. 381.

35. RV, p. 83.

36. Ibid., pp. 77–78.

37. Ibid., p. 84; Perry's italics.

38. GTV, p. 385; Perry's italics.

39. Ibid., chap. xxi.

40. RV, p. 53; Perry's italics.

41. Ibid., p. 84.

42. As Perry did, GTV, p. 616.

43. Ibid., pp. 656–68.

44. RV, p. 85; Perry's italics.

45. GTV, p. 617.

46. Ibid., p. 658.

47. Ibid., p. 386; Perry's quotes.

48. Ibid., p. 398–99.

49. Ibid., p. 385; Perry's quotes and italics.

50. RV, pp. 62–63.

51. Ibid., pp. 90–91.

52. Ibid., p. 91.

53. Ibid., p. 104.

54. Ibid., p. 93.

55. Ibid., p. 50.

56. Ibid., p. 91.

57. Ibid., pp. 94–96.

58. Ibid., p. 96.

59. Ibid., pp. 92–93; Perry's italics.

60. Ibid., p. 93.

61. Ibid., pp. 98–99.

62. Ibid., p. 82; Perry's quotes.

63. Ibid., p. 94; Perry's italics.

64. Ibid., p. 95; Perry's italics.

65. Ibid.

66. Ibid., p. 106.

67. Ibid., p. 95.

68. Joel Feinberg, "Naturalism and Liberalism in the Philosophy of Ralph Barton Perry" (Ph.D. diss., University of Michigan, 1957), p. 323.

69. Charles L. Stevenson, *Ethics and Language* (paperbound ed., New Haven: Yale University Press, 1960), pp. 270–71.

70. Cf. Moore, op. cit., p. 10 f., and RV, chap. 1, esp. pp. 9–11.

71. Moore, op. cit., esp. pp. 15–16.

72. Stevenson, loc. cit.

73. Ibid., p. 270; Stevenson's quotes and italics.

74. Ibid., and Feinberg, op. cit., p. 400.

Appendix to Chapter III

Summary Outline of Perry's Theory of Value

A. Value theories rejected:

The source of value is not to be found in the decrees of authority whether supernatural or supra-natural. Nor is it to be shrouded in the mysticism or obscurantism of divine inspiration or revelation or human intuition. There is an objective science of value.

B. Value as the object of any interest.

Value is any object of any interest.

1. Interest and Perry's view of man.

An interest is an attitude either positive–for equals good, or negative–against equals evil. An interest is an interest of an individual. Man is an interested animal. The individual man is the source of value.

2. Objects presented to interests–Perry's realism.

Only individuals think. A man does not have bare interests; he has interests in objects. His interest in an object involves his taking something to be an object. Cognition mediates interest. The realism of his interest depends upon the reality and realizability of the object, or the realism of his expectations.

C. Harmonious integration of interests–the individual.

Since man has many interests, the problem of value is not to find goods but to choose among them. He must organize his selection so as to maximize his good.

1. Criteria for integration.

Interests may be classified and ranked in several ways, chief among which are intensity, preference, and inclusiveness. While for all other criteria interests are only commensurable criterion by criterion, the principle of inclusiveness takes precedence in all ranking of values. That which would satisfy all interests—i.e., would be the most inclusive—provides the most value.

2. The process of rational reflection.

The individual is faced with the task of ordering his interests. His success is colored by the completeness of his awareness of his interests as well as the realism of the interests themselves. His problem is to so structure his interests as to reduce conflict and incompatibility of interests in favor of harmony. This involves rationalization in favor of the inclusiveness of the integration.

3. The inclusive self-interest.

Here the principle of harmonious integration of interests culminates for the individual in the marriage of the criterion of inclusiveness to rational reflection. The offspring is the interest of the individual in all of his interests. It is self-interest in the extreme. It asks what is best for the individual as a whole.

D. Harmonious integration of interests—among individuals.

The interests and thoughts of a group are those of the members of the group. There is no group mind. The problem is to replace conflict by the organization of these interests for the maximum good of all members.

1. Criteria broadened.

Again, there are several ways of classifying interests. The principle of inclusiveness still reigns supreme. It is now expanded to encompass the inclusive self-interests of individuals. That which would benefit the inclusive self-interests of all people is best.

2. The role of rational reflection.

The success of harmonious integration among individuals is colored by the extent to which those concerned are aware of their own inclusive self-interests as well as those of others. This requires openness and facility of communication and the willingness to co-operate in the pursuit of the highest level of self-interest satisfaction for all individuals.

3. The inclusive benevolent interest.

Since there is no group mind, a necessary condition for the realization of the *summum bonum* is that each individual have as part of his inclusive self-interest an interest in those of all others. The attitude of 'devil take the hindmost' is to be prevented by making concern for all, including the hindmost, an integral part of concern for self.

E. The egocentric predicament and Perry's theory of value.

This section represents the more general critique. Perry had two distinct problems: how to construe obligation in individual terms without appeal to external authority, and how to conceive recognition of the good in individual terms without falling into the abyss of vicious relativism. His theory of value represents the attempt to provide one solution to serve both problems.

1. The problem of knowing interests of others.

At any time there may be a considerable disparity between what an individual takes to be the interests of others and what they actually are. For this person, then, the question must arise as to the realism of his benevolent interest and therefore of his inclusive self-interest. To what extent can he account for interests of others as they are and to what extent is he forced to conceive these interests in his own mind? In effect, the question is raised in Perry's terms, 'How realistic is this theory of value considering the limitations on realism of the expectations of any individual about the interests of others?'

2. Is benevolence justified as a goal?

Of what use is the principle of benevolence to the theory? Does it represent any more than some sort of glue to bind the theory together and to keep it from flying apart toward the extremes of vicious relativism and imposition of external authority? Does it do any more than blur the distinction between the questions, 'What's in it for me?' and 'What's in it for everyone?' Can a democratic society survive without blurring these distinctions to some extent?

IV. Perry's Theory of Society

Suppose, without any pretense of a basis in adequate biography, that Perry had addressed himself directly to the consideration of some such question as 'What would be the best society?' This would have raised other questions as to the proper definition of 'best.' Indeed, this might have been viewed as the 'prior question.' In the light of his procedure in *The General Theory of Value* as well as in his other major publications, this would seem to be a fairly likely interpretation of Perry's intentions. For, his concern with the elucidation, defense and promotion of his conception of the ideal of democracy is present in all of them. And, in all of them his theory of value is used as the touch-stone for the critique of other theories of society as well as for the defense of his own theory of the ideal society.

Perry's theory of society is set forth and examined in three stages. The first represents a statement of his problem, as it were, as the search for the best society. Harmonious integration appears as the standard of evaluation and all non-democratic forms are found wanting. In the second stage Perry's view of democracy is developed through a discussion of American democracy and the puritan ideal, and with particular attention to his distinction between political and social democracy. It will probably not surprise anyone then to learn that he conceived democracy as harmonious integration. The third, and final, stage under the heading 'Making the theory work' involves a consideration of Perry's approach to the difficulties attending the practicability of the theory. If his theory of society was more or less a translation of his theory of value, then in this last stage the problems were essentially those of getting people to form or reform society in accordance with his theory of value.

Once again the issue must be raised over Perry's desire to do two things at one and the same time: to analyze and to persuade. Strictly speaking, theory of society and theory of value are not identical. One purports to elucidate the concept 'value' and the other to elucidate the concept 'society.' Perry did not define these terms identically. If anything, he wanted to define them so as to permit communication between them. His theory of value was to make a difference to the search for the best society, and a definition of society was required to permit the applicability of his theory of value in this quest. However, the development of certain aspects of his theory of value required, as was seen earlier, a particular conception of society. In effect these two theories were developed from their separate basic definitions along identical, or rather, intertranslatable lines. In the process Perry was engaged in 'explaining' value and society as they might be conceived. His identification of 'morality' with particular aspects of these theories suggests that he was bent on persuasion in addition to analysis. The distinction between these theories was thus confused.

Perry was not very helpful in resolving this confusion. In *Puritanism and Democracy* he spoke of the objectivity of his analysis in terms of the consistent application of a particular criterion and then proceeded to establish this criterion as his theory of the ideal society.[2] He insisted on the point that an ideal was truly worthy of efforts toward its atainment.[3] In *Realms of Value* he insisted that the analysis of value, morality and society made acceptance of democracy obligatory, i.e., as truly deserving allegiance.[4] However, the fact that he may have claimed too much for his theory of society need not detract from the overall merits of its proposal as a theory of society. But the further elaboration of these last points must await their turn in the discussion which may now begin.

The Search for the Best Society

Perry's theory of value and theory of society were based upon the same position regarding the nature of man and the condition of men vis à vis the universe. If value was to be examined on "the plane and in the contexts of physical nature," [5] so too was society. For, as he put it, "In its most general sense, 'society' names the fact that there is more than one human being in the world, and that the several human beings are related to one another." [6] The study of society, then, was to focus on human beings and their interrelationships. Supra-human entities or peculiar forces were viewed as irrelevant or misleading if the study of society was not to become bogged down in mysticism. Thus, for example, in maintaining that "a person is not a society, and a society is not a person," [7] he noted the following dangers:

> To conceive a society as a person literally and in all seriousness is doubly disastrous. It leads to idolatry, that is, the transfer to non-persons of the attitudes appropriate only to persons. It invests non-persons with a specious dignity, and leads to such distortions as ecclesiasticism

and statism. In the second place, to conceive society as a person stands in the way of understanding either personality or society. By resorting to metaphor and loose analogy it diverts attention away from the internal structure and dynamics of personal integration; away from the real locus of social integration, which derives interpersonal structures from the intrapersonal structures of its members.[8]

The second disaster refers not only to the effects of personification of 'society,' but to the notion of social force as well. The notion of some sort of disembodied social force to account for either the development of individual personality or for the character of interpersonal relations is at best useless and at worst a barrier to the advancement of knowledge of society. For the term social force stands for no more than an 'I know not what' sort of cause. It is about as useful as 'phlogiston' as an explanation of personality or human interaction. It is possible to use the term as shorthand for 'I know not what' while engaging in activities designed to clarify the investigation of human personality and human interrelationships. However, there is grave danger of falling into the assumption that because there is a name, the name has to stand for something and that to know the name is to know the something. The term 'social force' may be brandished as a weapon to bar the path of inquiry. Q. 'Why do people interact in a particular way?' A. 'There are social forces controlling their interactions.' Q. 'Why do opiates put one to sleep?' A. 'Opiates have dormative powers.' One may feel that he has been given an answer to his questions and be discouraged from pressing his inquiry.

Perry's concern to prevent this possibility was not just the concern of the scholar. The first disaster indicated above is closely related to the second. He wished to destroy any claim to legitimate or scientifically respectable support for the proponents of statism. The issue here is not whether these proponents actually believe in the mystique of the divine mission of the *Volk* or of materialistic determinism or even whether they encourage rigorous investigation of personality or social interaction. The issue for Perry was whether proponents of these views were to be permitted to claim justification of a scientific sort for the control and manipulation of human beings in the name of the inevitability of social forces or in the name of the supra-organic state.[9] As will be seen Perry's theories of society and of education take such roadblocks in the path of inquiry as roadblocks in the path to democracy. The first steps along this path required the exposition of a rational account of society.

Perry's analysis of society.—If society is not a person, it is still not a mere collection of persons. Society presumes organization. As a whole it is different from any of its parts. A society is a system, "its members occupy certain interrelated places or roles in the whole; and these roles can be abstracted from the individuals who occupy them." A human society in the "full sense of the term . . . is a society of persons united by the modes of interaction characteristic of persons."[10] The members share common knowledge and know that they share it. This is what Perry meant by "community of objects" and "communication."[11] Moreover, they share interests in common, and to greater or lesser extent, are aware of and are interested in one another's interests. They agree on common ends and co-operate in pursuit of these ends.[12]

One must be careful in reading Perry to watch out for the transition from the discussion of 'society' as a sort of general term and the sort of singular or particular historic society as in 'a society.' A society (to continue the exposition of Perry's view) is a "system of systems" whose uniqueness or singularity is reflected in the idiosyncratic character of a particular system or of the total pattern of systems as they are interrelated.[13] Thus, "using the term 'culture' to embrace any acquired peculiarity, it is assumed that a singular society must possess *some* cultural idiosyncracy." [14]

The idea that the uniqueness of a society is based on *acquired* peculiarity is pointed up in Perry's conception of social institutions. The chief distinction between 'society' and 'social institution' is that the latter is equivalent to a subsystem of a society in the fuller sense of the term. In other words "an institution is a kind of a society," [15] or a sub-society defined in the same manner as any other kind of society, even the system of systems which denote such singular societies as America or England. The importance of this point for Perry is brought out in the following passages.

An institution is a social structure organized by men for the sake of a purpose which it serves. In other words, an institution is *instituted*. Though it may have been anticipated by nature, it is reaffirmed and maintained by culture. Thus the political institution of government can be traced back to the fact that by virtue of their comparative power or self-assertiveness one or more individuals of a group possess a natural ascendancy over their fellows: but the institution begins when this control is recognized, accepted, and perpetuated as a social utility. Though it may have arisen, and may be perpetuated, by habit and instinct, an institution is endorsed by the wills of its members, who identify it with their interests.

So to conceive an institution is to identify an institution with its rationale, rather than with the accidents of its origin. It is a social organization which members of a society justify to themselves as useful and good. They say, in effect, that if they did not happily possess such an institution they would inaugurate one. And the purpose which is served by the exercise of its function provides the standard by which they reshape and seek to perfect it.[16]

To conceive social organization in terms of its rationale as Perry has done is to assert, in effect, that societies are instituted by men for men. For if any institution can be so viewed, then so too can the system which includes them. Society can continue as a more or less rationally organized conglomeration of subsystems or it can be more rationally organized. One can criticize the rationale of any given society by the standard of the purpose for having society and restructure society in accordance with the most rational organization for the pursuit of that purpose. In whatever manner society began, it was fashioned by men to serve their purposes. It can be refashioned.

What Perry was saying was that an institution is an institution by virtue of its justification. Even the reason 'We have always done so' is a justification according to the belief that it is 'good for us to do what we have always done.' Even the rule of the most powerful and aggressive may seem justified by the belief that it is better to be thus ruled and live than to fight it and die. The ruler might even try to create the belief in his subjects that this is the best form of social organization in their own interests. Perry's point was that there must be some belief that an institution serves a socially beneficial purpose for an institution to exist.

This leaves any institution open to criticism of its raison d'être on two counts: first, is it as socially beneficial as it could be; and second, how reasonable or rational is the argument for its existence as it stands? In sum, is it worthy of the belief that it is good or must it be changed? If this is appropriate for the criticism of any institution, then it is appropriate for the criticism of the entire system of institutions.

Now it must be clearly understood that Perry was more a philosopher than a social scientist. His analysis of 'society' may seem a bit facile or cavalier in the sweep of its generalizations. One might be quick to point out, for example, that the purposes of individuals in playing a particular institutional role may differ greatly and that there may be little clear recognition of the value to all members of society in insuring that the role continue to be played. Indeed Perry was concerned to encourage the work of the social scientists in bringing such factors to the surface in order that the members of society might more adequately assess their institutions. The major concern for Perry in theory of society was not with the definition of society per se but with the delineation and defence of his conception of the best society. He needed a conception of society which would permit the most incisive criticism of alternative forms of social organization if he were to point the way to the best forms.

Harmonious integration as the criterion.—One is tempted to say that in the search for the best society, theory of society as it has been developed in the discussion thus far was an introduction. It might be taken as a prolegomenon to the major business of the criticism of existing social institutions and of the development of a conception of the ideal society. Thus, one might want to say that, after all, theory of society is one thing and the judgment of the merits of particular social organizations is another. To say something about how societies operate is far different from saying whether they operate well, or, indeed, whether they ought to be permitted to operate as they do, or even how they ought to operate ideally.

While granting that these considerations involve different sorts of judgments, Perry insisted that theory of society included all of these sorts of judgments. For Perry, the critique of 'society' included the criticism of various forms of social organization. Perhaps it would be more appropriate to say that Perry was more concerned with the development and test of his theory of the ideal society than of his theory of society *per se*. At any rate it is clear that he denied this sort of distinction.[17]

It is not crucial to determine here whether Perry was correct in so doing. But, it is important to note that he was no longer concerned merely with whether his theory of society was adequate as a characterization of social organization. Rather, the question became 'How, ideally, ought social organization to be characterized?' This introduced the moral standard into theory of society. And, the moral standard was the principle of harmonious happiness or harmonious integration. Perry wanted to establish this standard as *the* moral standard. He posed his problem as follows:

If harmonious happiness can be truly affirmed to be the moral standard, it must so agree with human nature and the circumstances of human life that men can adopt it by education, persuasion, and choice; and having adopted it, can govern their conduct in accordance with its requirements. It must be qualified to serve as a criterion by which human interests, acts, characters, and organizations can be classified and ranked. The evidence that it satisfied these requirements will be found in the fact that it is so adopted and employed.

If, however, harmonious happiness is to be proved to be *the* moral standard, to the exclusion of other standards for which a similar claim is made, it must possess further and unique qualifications. Otherwise it will be merely one standard among many, differing only historically. There would be no ground of persuasion by which the adherent of another standard could be converted to this standard. It could be judged *in terms of* this standard, but there could be no judgment between them. The standard of harmonious happiness would have no *theoretical* precedence.[18]

Clearly, Perry wanted to do more than point out the differences between the principle of harmonious happiness and the other moral standards. To say that a given standard is uniquely qualified as *the* moral standard is to say that it is superior to any other standard. What were its qualifications? "In the first place, the standard of harmonious happiness is capable of being agreed on—both theoretically and practically. . . . " In the second place "it embraces all interests, [and therefore] is to *some extent* to everybody's interest. . . . " And finally, it "is the only norm which is capable of appealing to all men not only severally but jointly. It is the only norm which promises benefits to each interest *together with* all other interests. It does not rob Peter to pay Paul, but limits Peter in order to pay both Peter and Paul." [19] It would appear that it is uniquely qualified as the moral standard because it is the standard of harmonious happiness.

Perhaps it is a bit unfair to Perry to put matters in this fashion. But, he was the one who raised the problem of the obligation to accept this as *the true standard*. In his efforts to establish the superiority of this standard Perry sought to prove that it alone of the standards which he had examined was consistent with a particular conception of proof. It is one thing to construct a standard to meet particular qualifications; it is quite another matter to prove that these qualifications ought to be met. Thus, for example, one might set out to prove that the adoption of the principle of harmonious happiness as *the* moral standard would be the best guarantor of impartiality or fairness to all persons. In support of this he might point out that in operation the principle denies any claims of particular individuals or agencies to private access to knowledge and/or proof of what would be best for all people. He does not thereby prove that guaranteeing impartiality of consideration of all interests or impariality in considering all people as sources of knowledge of interests ought to be criteria for the identification of the superior moral standard. Perry's introduction of the principle of harmonious happiness into his theory of society as *the* moral standard constituted his *assertion* that men, individually and in concert, were to determine the merits of their own institutions. He asserted that these institutions were to be judged by men according to their conduciveness to the well-being of men.[20]

The two chief criteria that Perry advanced for the evaluation of the social benefit of an institution were the criteria of "universality" and "liberality."[21] Taken together they comprise social well-being as defined by the principle of harmonious integration. They represent what Perry referred to as "universalistic individualism."[22] Any institution of a society is to be judged in accordance with the questions 'Are as many individuals as possible benefited or does this institution provide exclusively for the benefit of only a few people?' 'Are the interests of each person given maximum room and support for satisfaction or does this institution limit them more than they need be limited?' As Perry noted "these are the canons ordinarily invoked by social reformers—who complain that the institution is 'harsh,' or restrictive of freedom to a degree not required for order and justice; or too narrow and exclusive in its jurisdiction."[23]

This did not mean that every institution must benefit all in exactly the same way. It might very well be the case that certain institutions best serve the over-all interests of the members of a society by being limited in application. Not everyone benefits in precisely the same way from public nursery schools or from boys' clubs. Still it might be in the interests of all to cater to the interests of those eligible to participate in the direct benefits of these institutions. The well-being of society is to be measured against the greatest possible benefit for all its members. The task is to structure society so as to provide for the highest level of well-being of each member consistent with that of every other member. This was the highest good as defined by the principle of harmonious integration of interests among individuals. This was what Perry called the *final end* of an institution and of society.[24] The search for the best society, then, involved above all else the judgment and evaluation of institutions in the light of this final end.

Rejection of non-democratic forms.—An organized society is not defined by the form of its government; government is only one of the institutions of a society. Nevertheless, the form of government has a great deal to do with the attainment of the over-all purpose or final end of society. Perry stated that "if organized society is to serve its purpose, there must be an over-all public policy, that is, a policy for all." Organized society required polity, "an over-all plan adopted by all for all, and imposed by all on all." Its purpose is "to create harmonious happiness by the adoption of a common plan," and "polity exists when such a plan is adopted and its fruits [are] enjoyed." [25] Clearly, whatever the actual form of a government, it could not be consistent with Perry's view of polity if it did not conduce to the operation of harmonious integration of interests.

Government of the many by an individual or by a few in the interest of harmonious happiness, as Perry conceived it, would be inconsistent with his conception of polity. One cannot justify such a government by divine right. This would presume a source of value superior to man. One cannot justify such government as in the interest of the state. The state has no interests; only people have interests. One cannot justify such a government as in the interest of the people. The interests of the people are what they take them to be and not what others take them to be. This does not mean that each and every institution has to be democratic in its organization, and that every individual has to be actively engaged in the forming of all decisions of government, or that the government should be the rule of the mass rather than the rule of the wise.[26] In any complex society authority must be delegated in the interest of efficiency. This is not efficiency for its own sake, but efficiency for the sake of promoting over-all well being. Some institutions as, for example, an army may function best if authority is delegated from the top down. Again, in a large society social well-being may be maximized by the efficiency of the delegation of authority to elected representatives who will be released from other activities to represent the interests of their constituents. However, these public servants do not have any right to rule that is not delegated by the people for whom they are to rule.

Sovereignty, in this view, rests with the people. They are to be seen as delegating authority not to rule over them but to rule for them. The executive and the legislator must answer to the people when the question of the justification of their actions is called. They must be responsive to the demands of the people in framing their actions. They can claim no privileged knowledge of the interests of the people. In the end the people must have the final say even if this consent is tacit. Still, government must provide "for channels by which the governed may voice their own interest. . . . " The people are to be "given a hearing; and in order to assure their being heard they are given the power to challenge, remove and replace their representatives—when these prove to be hard of hearing." [27]

The particular form of government in any given society might not appear to be as important as the existence of such safeguards. However, one is forced to observe that whatever the legal form of government, if it provides for these safeguards it is in fact a democratic government. In asserting the principle of harmonious happiness as the criterion for the evaluation of polity, Perry rejected non-democratic government out of hand. What else could one conclude from such a statement as the following: "Polity as a morally justifiable institution rests on the thoughtful agreement of those who live under it: a coöperative organization entered into by persons in whom the interests of all overrule the interests of each." [28] It is not a very large step from this to the assertion that the democratic forms of government are suited par excellence as the ideal forms of government. Before taking this step with Perry one might do well to get a clearer conception of Perry's view of democracy.

Perry's View of Democracy

There were two strands introduced in the discussion of the rejection of non-democratic forms which are now to be picked up and developed as central to Perry's conception of democracy. The first of these involves the tension between the rule of the many and the rule of the wise. The second involves his view of democracy as more than a form of government, but, indeed, as a way of life. It will then be possible to show just how Perry construed democracy, ideally, as harmonious integration in operation.

American democracy and the puritan ideal.—In his *Puritanism and Democracy* Perry stated at the outset that his analysis of American democracy was to be understood as an essay in history for a particular purpose. He had chosen to examine puritanism and democracy as basic philosophical orientations and apologia influential in the formation of the United States and in the development of that nation to the present time. Perry did not deny other influences but contended that an understanding of this development would be deficient without proper attention to these.[29]

Had it been the whole of his purpose to contribute something to the discussion of the American mind or character— a subject of particular interest to Perry, by the way [30]—this work would have some, but scarcely as much, relevance to the present consideration as it does. That American democracy could have developed from two such seemingly incompatible seeds as the ideal of equality and the ideal of puritanism suggests some sort of integration and interpenetration of these ideals. But Perry did more than unravel the character of this integration and interpenetration; he applied the standard of harmonious happiness to these ideals in order to indicate how they ought to be integrated. Perry did not find the ideal character of American democracy in the integration of these ideals; rather he attempted to integrate these ideals into a conception of American democracy as he thought it ought ideally to be conceived.[31]

Puritanism taught that conscience and private judgment were to be respected above authority. It insisted on measurement by moral standards and in terms of higher good. It preached a doctrine of progress to the higher good. It favored the subordination of some interests in the interest of the greater well-being of the individual. But it was a greater well-being to be enjoyed in a life after this life and not during this life.[32] As Perry pointed out, puritanism was not an unmixed blessing:

There are certain ingredients in which the puritan mixture is deficient, or which it omits altogether. For lack of these things even the good ingredients lose their flavor and the dish is bitter to the taste. The puritan saw a limited truth, and what he saw was distorted because of what he failed to see. This distorted puritanism consisted of a narrow preoccupation with morality to the exclusion of the graciousness and the beauty of life; a pharisaical emphasis on the letter of the rule at the expense of its spirit; evil imagination; prudishness and canting humility; a hard repression of all spontaneities and all natural impulses, resulting in the masking of real motives by virtuous and edifying pretension; a morbid habit of introspection; censoriousness; hardness, intolerance, and an aversion to joy, especially the joy of other people; obsequious submission to a cruel and despotic God, and through preoccupation with the moral law a neglect of those aspects which nature and the universe present to the senses, the affections, and the reason.[33]

Essentially, this view of man emphasizes his capacity for baseness and depravity while holding out to the few who are fit for it the promise of salvation—that through divine grace the baseness and depravity may be overcome and heaven awaits them. While it insists on the importance of individual conscience it dwells on the limits of most men to attain good conscience. Moreover, in the end it tends to intolerance and theocracy, the rule of the religious elect.[34]

If puritanism takes, on the whole, a rather pessimistic view of man and his capacities, democracy takes a rather optimistic view of things. The egalitarian view of man also recognizes the inherent differences of men but emphasizes the superiority of man over the other forms of life. It is an optimistic view which presumes that all men have been fitted with the minimum tools of intellect required for the management of their interests and that it is possible to narrow the differences of men by education.[35] Perry saw American democracy as an egalitarian view of man qualified by elements of puritanism. The chief qualification was that the narrowing of the differences between men should involve levelling up to the best which each man can attain. This was not an unbridled faith in the superiority of the common. It was a faith in the ability of the common to contribute to the construction of superiority.[36] This faith was embodied in Perry's contention that "every individual is a potential vehicle of truth on any matter to which he directs his cognitive faculties. Democracy seeks a government by enlightenment, and bestows political power on all individuals insofar as they are sources of light; which every individual is, for anything that one can know in advance to the contrary." [37]

And here lay Perry's answer to the question of whether the many or the wise should rule. American democracy as he saw it could not support a naive egalitarianism which might demand the conformity of all with the norm of mediocrity or the level of the lowest. He could not accept as genuine a pseudo-democracy subject to the sway of the demagogue. As he put it: "Democracy is concerned to develop and liberate the faculties of its people, and to provide those faculties with the data suitable to their exercise, submitting itself to such beliefs as may then emerge." [38]

The notion of submission to beliefs introduces another element of puritanism in American democracy. But, it was not submission to belief in the dogma of puritanism. It was submission to belief in a higher good of man here on earth. It was submission of selfish interest to the public interest through unanimous belief in the process of agreement.

Perry stated that the "fundamental agreement is that there should be a state at all with power of coercion over its members." So long as it is remembered that the purpose of government is to serve the interests of man then he "who belongs to a dissenting minority today may cherish a hope of belonging to the triumphant majority of tomorrow." [39] For, the majority rule in a democracy is not the alignment of the party of the many against the party of the few, but a device for reaching decisions on courses of action where action is required. A democratic government does not require unanimity on each decision but only an agreement as to the basic procedure for reaching decisions in the interest of all its members. (The difficulties attending this position will be examined more closely later on.)

This was instrumental to the other element of puritanism in the ideal of American democracy as Perry would have it. This was the notion of progress toward the higher good of man, only not, as in puritanism, a higher good after life on earth, but rather for men here on earth. Perry summed this up as follows:

> Puritanism is the exponent of the harsh necessities of the moral life. Morality is essentially the imposing of a form of personal integrity and social justice upon the natural life of man. But morality has no justification

except in terms of that very natural life to which it does violence. . . . Puritanism sees that life must be curtailed, to which democracy adds, 'in order that it may abound.' [40]

This brings up the discussion of the relationship between political and social democracy.

Political and social democracy.—The right to vote might be a symbol of democracy, but it may be an empty symbol. If those who have the vote do not have the ability or the opportunity to make decisions, the right is meaningless. If they do not have the intelligence and background to make democracy work, its name may stand as a shell or veneer to cover up some other form of rule. If people cannot order their affairs to provide the bare necessities of life, they may fall prey to those who promise to do it for them. If they can cooperate only in an attempt to secure the minima, they may sustain existence but they do not improve it. The purpose of social organization, according to Perry, was to improve existence and not just to sustain it.

Political democracy without social democracy would not work. Social democracy without some form of political democracy would be impossible. For Perry, the genius of the ideal of American democracy lay in insistence upon this point.[41] Political democracy was concerned with who should rule and how they should rule; social democracy was concerned with the purpose for which they should rule. Political democracy, to survive, required at least the continuing desire of individuals to protect their interests against the encroachments of other individuals. The laws, regulations, and institutional forms of government could not be viewed as so sacred as to be unalterable.

Perry decried this sort of ecclesiasticism and noted that the instruments of political democracy were to be criticized and justified by their conduciveness to social democracy. Laws are formed in the light of conditions obtaining at the time they are formed. Lawmakers cannot predict the future. As conditions change with time, old laws may work new hardships.[42] Advances in technology and change in the structure of the economy may make people increasingly dependent upon others for the access to the means of their subsistence. Intimidation and control of individuals becomes an economic and political possibility. As social organization becomes more complex, education is required to help each individual to understand the organization in order that he might hope to determine where his interests lie. Social democracy as a set of attitudes is required to insure that the proper courses are open and may be taken to make political democracy work.[43]

Social democracy would be little more than a cry of pain without political democracy. There must be institutions through which the attitudes of social democracy can be asserted. Perry contended that "democracy in its fundamental, modern, and American meaning, is the application of moralism to human institutions, and in particular to political institutions." [44] Or, as he had also put it: "The reasons by which democracy or any other form of state is justified must be derived from the reasons by which the state itself is justified. If democracy is the best state, it must be because democracy is pre-eminently, what the state as such is designed to be." [45] This was not, however, an attempt to blur the distinction between political and social democracy. Rather, Perry insisted on the distinction between "democracy as a political means and democracy as a social end." [46] His contention was that only through some form of political democracy could one hope to advance the end of social democracy.

The issue here focuses on Perry's attempt to clarify the business of evaluating particular institutions of government as democratic or non-democratic. He wanted to point out that there was nothing inherently more democratic or undemocratic in a 'government which governs least' or in a 'welfare state.' So long as it is borne in mind that the purpose of having a state is to advance the welfare of the people, the form of government which might best support this goal may be different for different groups of people in the light of the peculiarities of their histories and conditions.[47] Social democracy was a cult of freedom. But, Perry saw two sides of freedom: "freedom from" and "freedom for."[48] Social democracy was not the ideal of the least harm to each individual; it was the ideal of the greatest good for each individual in keeping with the greatest good of every other individual. It called for the development of the capabilities of all individuals in order that the best interests that each individual might have would be represented as best they could by each individual in the democratic arena.[49]

The measure of democracy was not the absence of restraint, but the presence of encouragement and the active promotion of the greatest good for all of society. For a given society, the style of political expression along a continuum between the poles suggested above would best be determined through the practical experience of that society. What might be the most efficient organization toward the goal of social democracy for one society might not be for another. The best society was not describable in minute detail but only within the general outlines of an ideal, the ideal of harmonious integration.

Democracy as harmonious integration—full circle.—Perry's theory of society, as his theory of what society ought to be, was democracy conceived in accordance with the principle of harmonious integration among individuals. But let Perry speak for himself here:

Democracy is the social application of this principle, and it shows the same universality. In its fundamental meaning a democracy is a society of persons who so manage their relations and their affairs as to escape the evils of isolation, frustration, and violence, and achieve the good of living innocently and fruitfully together. It is a harmony of wills by which to achieve the maximum fulfillment of the interests of all concerned. So defined the democratic society is the ideal society, and in proportion as this ideal is achieved a society merits the name of democracy.[50]

But, this was precisely what one would have expected. For Perry to have come to any other conclusion would have been rather peculiar indeed. 'Best' was defined in social terms. His theory of value and theory of society proceeded from the same assumptions. He applied the principles of his theory of value as the standard by which to evaluate alternative forms of social organization. His theory of value embraced a particular sort of social organization in the very definition of that standard. In effect, Perry's theory of the ideal society was a translation of key aspects of his theory of value into the vernacular of theory of society. This has been apparent, perhaps painfully so considering the extent of the repetition involved, in the discussion of his theory of society to this point.

The canons of universality and liberality as noted earlier comprised his principle of harmonious integration of interests. The first of these, universality, was the translation of inclusiveness into a conception of fairness. The second, liberality, was the translation of maximization of good into Perry's conception of freedom for, or positive freedom. The first refers to the democratic principle of equal consideration; the second, to the social ideal of the promotion of the greatest good for all. They tempered one another in Perry's social philosophy in such a way as to make the greatest good for all identical with the outcomes of the equal consideration of the interests of all. Two difficulties are worth noting at this point.

First, equal consideration, as Perry used it, tends to identify interest in maximizing good for all and interest in agreement. This is the same problem raised in the discussion of his theory of value. Perry did not want a system of morality based upon selfishness. The greatest good for all, as he saw it, required the curbing of the selfish activities of certain members of society in the interests of all members. In what sense can it be said that this is actually in the interest of those members whose activities have been thus limited? How can they be shown that this is in their interest? To show that this sort of agreement would be prudent is to suggest that there might be times when it would not be prudent. It would be to play their own game by trying to make them see 'what's in it for them.'

Perry's treatment of the topic of punishment and persuasion shows his practicality in taking account of such people. However, he insisted, and he had to insist to be consistent, that in the ideal society punishment would be uncalled for. Punishment was reserved for the immoral. He defined morality in a manner which made such people immoral. In effect, in pursuing selfish ends at the expense of other ends of members of society, they had placed themselves outside society as enemies. On Perry's view no one had the right to place himself outside society. Rights are defined by morality.[51] The ideal or moral society approached realization as all of its members became moral. In the ideal society those who acted solely for selfish interests could not exist as members. If such people do exist, the critique of society by the standards of the ideal requires their reformation or elimination. They must see their personal interests as a part of total social well-being in such a way as to make the result of inter-personal agreement the court of last resort for the definition of personal interest. They have to believe in fairness and agree to agree.[52]

The second difficulty revolves about Perry's conception of freedom. This was the extension into theory of society of his position that positive interests in objects cannot be translated into negative interests in the absence or destruction of objects. Once again it may be said that there is nothing in logic to prohibit this sort of translation. There was, however, a persuasive element in Perry's insistence on the distinction between 'freedom from' and 'freedom for' or 'to.'

Consider the hypothetical case of two boys, one from a comfortable middle class suburban community and the other from a less favored neighborhood. Suppose further that the latter, as a consequence of his circumstances, is ignorant of the opportunities and interests that he might pursue and perhaps satisfy with advanced education. No one is holding him back purposefully. There are no laws or regulations that deny him a college education. All he has to do is pass the same entrance examinations as the other boy. The questions are whether he would even think of trying to pass them and whether if he were to try he would be adequately prepared to do so. He is free from legal restraint, yet because of his ignorance and background he is not as free to develop his capacities as the other boy.

One can list the factors in the less favored boy's background as limitations of his freedom. He is not free *from* ignorance. He is not free *from* a particular sub-cultural value system. Or, with Perry, one may want to say that he is not free *to* develop his capacities. 'Freedom from' emphasizes restraints or negative interests. It looks to the removal of barriers. 'Freedom to' or 'for,' emphasizes positive interests. It looks to the construction of pathways to goals. While a man may not be free from restraint where there is no pathway, the impact of positive freedom is in its emphasis upon maximizing goods rather than on limiting evils. As it is easily seen these are not so logically distinct as Perry would have them. But there is a difference in persuasive impact. A philosophy intent on promoting the maximization of good wants to make the positive impact implicit in 'freedom for.'

Once again the consistency of Perry's translation of theory of value into theory of the ideal society is clear. And, if one accepts his theory of value, he also accepts this translation of his theory of value. The significant distinction between these theories lay in the greater attention to the practical problems of complex social interaction in the theory of the ideal society. A look at his approach to these problems will afford the opportunity for a closer examination of his basic position.

Making the Theory Work

To present a picture of society as it ought to be is far different from picturing society as it is. There is a presumption that some aspects of society might require change if there is to be movement in the direction of the ideal. Existing conditions, including attitudes, have to be taken into account. The practical problems that these conditions place in the way of realizing the ideal must be faced. If Perry's theory of the ideal society was to have any practical significance, certain attitudes had to be implanted in the individual members of society. If the ideal society was actually to function, the citizen of that society had to meet certain qualifications. If the society was to be realized, a particular conception of progress had to hold sway. If this sort of society was truly the ideal society, then it had to be the ideal for all peoples. These were Perry's chief requirements for the application of his theory to the real world of men and nations. In effect, he outlined a set of tasks.

The problem of commitment to ideals.—Other things being equal, the extent of the realization of the ideal society depends upon the extent to which the members of society are committed to its realization. This is a truism of such sort as 'nothing succeeds like success.' It is an extension of James' *Will to Believe.*[53] It is a built-in requirement of Perry's theory.

If social organization is what people make it, and if the ideal social organization is what people might make it, then the commitment of people to the ideal is required to bring it about, or, if it should exist to some extent, to maintain it and develop it. Perry's theory requires the willingness to work co-operatively for the benefits of co-operation. The ideal society, on this view, *is* the society of co-operating individuals. It can exist and/or endure only to the extent that its members believe in co-operation.

When all believe in something they are said to be of common persuasion with respect to that belief. The problem is to get them to be of common persuasion. It is of little practical help to say that when they are so persuaded the ideal may have been realized. The problem is to insure that they will be. It may not be enough to call them immoral for not being so persuaded. The problem is to get them to accept the particular view of morality and to act in accordance with it. In sum the practical problem *is* to persuade them.

Democracy according to Perry is an ideology; "it defines an order of values which pervades all of the major aspects of human life." [54] As such it requires faith, but a peculiar sort of faith, a faith that will not tolerate dogmatism or fanaticism. It is a faith in human reason. He advanced his position as follows:

It is characteristic of democracy, in this broad sense, that its adherents are not merely loyal to it but believe that its claims to acceptance are superior to those of any rival ideology. It is considered a mark of enlightment in the modern age to adopt an attitude of sceptical relativism toward one's fundamental allegiance—whether it be to God, or to country, or to any other cause. The effect is strangely paradoxical. He who claims for his cause that it is in some sense true or valid offers reasons for it. He, on the other hand, who claims nothing for his cause save that it is his, looks to no proof save his own sheer assertion. Hence sceptical relativism generates fanaticism. Such fanaticism is the most terrible of all fantacisms: since it is incorrigible and remorseless. It is blind to evidence and deaf to argument. Against opposing doctrines it brings a closed mind and a naked will. It submits to no arbitration but that of force. Its only credential is its power to survive, and the authenticity of its credentials is established by its success in surviving. It consecrates itself, therefore, to the cultivation of power and to the destruction of its rivals.

The adherent of democracy rejects sceptical relativism and claims truth. He refuses to concede that democracy is just one among conflicting ideologies, each of which is good for its own devotees. He claims it is the optimum form of social organization, endorsed by advancing enlightenment and acceptable even to present opponents in proportion as their ignorance, inexperience or willful perversity is overcome; in proportion, that is, as it finds entrance into thoughtful and disinterested minds.[55]

Now one may or may not like the force of Perry's remarks about sceptical relativism, but the impact of these remarks is clear. Even the sceptical relativist has faith in a position. Even if he does not subscribe to the fanaticism to which Perry felt it must lead, he takes a stand. And such a stand Perry could not tolerate. For, in the end it leads to either of two alternatives which he could not accept. Either all ideologies have an equal claim to truth or no ideology can make a claim to truth.

The first of these alternatives is patently unacceptable if one wants to mean anything at all by 'truth.' One may not know for sure which one of a group of conflicting beliefs is true, but at least one does know that if they do conflict they cannot all be true. For otherwise, believing is all that is necessary to the certification of truth. And, in that case, the word 'truth' becomes so much excess baggage in human language except as a tool in the hands of the proselytizer.

In the case of the second alternative it seems clear that Perry's assessment was accurate. So long as human life does require organization it will be organized. If it is to sustain itself at all there must be some means of insuring order. So long as conflicting ideologies do abound and contend with one another, there must be some means of protecting a given society against the encroachments of the ideologies of another or some means of enforcing allegiance to a favored ideology to prevent the breakdown of order through moral anarchy. Where no claim can be made for the truth of any ideology the obvious alternatives for insuring order are agreement or force. This is not, by the way, to deny the importance of tradition in insuring order. It goes behind tradition and asks of any given society which of the two alternatives is most strongly represented in its traditions.

The problem of commitment to belief in democracy was for Perry identical with the problem of commitment to belief in any area of concern. Thus with regard to the critique of cultures he stated: "Cultural relativism or solipsism in the vicious sense cannot be stated without self-contradiction. As has so often been pointed out, the reflective act by which a relativity is discovered surmounts the relativity which is asserted." And, he continued: "The development of cultural critique follows the same course as the development of all knowledge." [56] "The fundamental maxim of knowledge," according to Perry, *"is to know as well as possible what there is to be known."* The chief supposition here is that there is a something to be known; that "in its dedication to truth science defers to things as they are, independent of human subjectivity." [57]

This reaffirmation of realism coming as it did toward the close of his career was still not an affirmation of naïve realism. All knowledge, all judgments are fallible. Perry held that, "although there is no such thing as an infallible cognition, and no such thing as a true judgment which *may* not be erroneous, it is legitimate to speak of a minimum of fallibility." [58] Scientific proof and scientific certainty he recognized as stemming from a subjective criterion, the absence of doubt. However, doubt was to be removed by evidence and when thus removed judgment might assume the form of commitment—"a knowledge on which to stake one's fortunes." [59]

Perry's view of commitment to democracy was founded essentially in the notion that a society exists for the welfare of all who comprise it and that no one or few of them have special access to the knowledge of the interests of all of them. The democratic persuasion was the persuasion that each man is to be taken as the best representative of his own interests and that, accordingly, each man has a stake in the determination of the overall interests of society.

However, it went further than this. As he saw things, while "there is no morally justifiable claim of one man or one group to rule over another, . . . there is a morally justifiable claim of the whole to rule over one of its parts." [60] Still there remains the practical problem of dealing with the one who by word or action refuses to be one of the parts, i.e., refuses to be persuaded.

The democratic citizen.—To the question 'Who is the democratic citizen?' the answer might be given quite simply as 'One who believes in democracy.' Belief in the idea of democracy is not demonstrated, however, merely by the tendency to spout the catch-phrases or slogans of liberty, fraternity, and equality. Belief in democracy is demonstrated in the propensity to act in accordance with the principle of harmonious happiness or harmonious integration. For Perry, the epitome of the democratic citizen was the harmoniously integrated person participating in the harmonious integration of society. However, such a person was committed by definition, to the rule of reason in personal as well as social integration. Perry put the matter as follows:

> When democracy is taken to mean the rule of people, and the term 'people' is taken to mean the mass or the mass mentality its refutation is self-evident. If democracy means the rule of those who are unfit to rule, it is condemned by definition. Instead of being the best form of society it is clearly the worst. If the rule of the people is to be justified, they must be believed to be the *best* qualified to rule—not necessarily well qualified, but at any rate the least disqualified.[61]

Perry's apparently guarded optimism here was not a grudging optimism. Nor, on the other hand, was it the naïve optimism of a *Candide*. Believing in the qualification of the people for rule did not make them qualified. His view was optimistic not in its description of what men were like, but in its confidence in what men could be like. It was a confidence in what men by co-operative endeavor could do for themselves. Somehow the ability as well as the desire to cooperate had to be developed in the people. Men are different and have different capacities. However, an optimistic view insists that these differences in capacities are not great enough to warrant the rule of the more able over the less able. There is one qualifying provision: the abilities of all people have to be developed as fully as possible.[62]

Thus, for example, there may be a difference in the potentialities of two individuals for the rational ordering of their individual interests and for participation in discussion and reasoned debate. Still if these potentalities are developed and realized at the highest level for each person, then the interests of each may be the most adequately represented in discussion. The presumption here, is that the inherent differences between individuals are not so great as environmental factors make them. Whether this is true or not, there is more good, as Perry defined good, to be gained from proceeding as though it were true then in presuming that it is not. At any rate, such optimism favors the deferment of judgment until after the attempt at improvement. And this attempt was the second task in the construction of democracy.

The notion of progress.—It was not enough for Perry that the democratic citizen be as reasonable and realistic as he could be. One may be reasonable and selfish. The selfish man is often quite realistic. Only then he is more likely to be called calculating. Perry wanted his citizen to be benevolent.

Now, no one has to be benevolent just because he is reasonable. There is a peculiarity of ordinary language which tends to blur this point. A person who listens to reason or is reasonable is taken to be the sort of person who is prepared to come to agreement with others. A man who is not so prepared is often characterized as unreasonable. One cannot reason with him, i.e., one cannot get him to come to agreement. The presumption is that if he is truly reasonable, he must see his obligation to come to agreement with others. He must be an 'agreeable' sort of person. But, where does this obligation come from?

For Perry it came from an acceptance of the ideal of democracy. The question is why anyone else should see the ideal as he did. Even the argument that everyone ought to be as reasonable as he can to protect and develop his own interests, does not place any obligation on the members of society to help one another develop their abilities to reason. Of course, they may be willing to accept this obligation in the interest of private gain, as for example, in the interest of benefiting by new inventions and conveniences. But this is not benevolence. According to Perry it was not an interest in progress either, or else it was a narrow and partial interest.

Progress, or social progress as Perry conceived it, included benevolence. In its broadest sense progress was measured by the standards of the ideal community. Advances in technology were not the measures of progress. The true measure lay in the benefit of invention and organization for the members of society as a whole. Does the new technique conduce to the advancement of the well-being of the members of society? Had fire been used only for destructive purposes its discovery would not have been a sign of progress. The development of atomic power as a means of destruction might have been a technological advance but whether or not the development of atomic power contributes to progress on the broader view remains to be seen. It must serve the positive end of promoting social well-being.[63]

Not only did Perry put progress in human terms; he put it in human hands. Progress was not something that happened to people or somehow had to happen to people as controlled by some sort of historic destiny. Progress in its broadest sense was something that people had to work for. While noting that there were many points of difference between his *Realms of Value* and Karl Popper's *The Open Society and Its Enemies*, Perry cited the "fundamental bond of agreement" [64] between these works. The agreement is symbolized in the following passage from Popper:

> To progress is to move toward some kind of end, towards an end which exists for us as human beings. 'History' cannot do that; only we, the human individuals, can do it; we can do it by defending and strengthening those democratic institutions upon which freedom, and with it progress, depends. And we shall do it much better as we become more fully aware of the fact that progress rests with us, with our watchfulness, with our efforts, with the clarity of our conception of our ends, and with the realism of their choice.[65]

The issue is not whether things happen to individuals over which they have no control. The issue is over the definition of progress as the increasing control by individuals acting in concert over the influences and factors impinging upon and contributing to their greatest well-being. The promotion in individuals of this kind of awareness, of this conception of progress was yet another practical task stemming from Perry's theory of the ideal society.

World in conflict.—Was it right for the United States to coerce the Japanese into surrender at the close of World

War II with the threat of further atomic bombing? The ideal form of social organizaiton, if it was *the ideal*, had, on Perry's view, to be the ideal for all nations. All people were to see it as true. The defeat of Japan was justified by the ideal. The Japanese people would be better off with a democratic society. The people of the world would be benefited more by the defeat and reformation of the Japanese than by the continuation of hostilities. The rationale for this position is summed up in the following:

Threatening war in order to prevent war, or making war to end war, is psychologically treacherous, but it is not morally contradictory. Harmonious happiness as a goal to be achieved by the organization of nations and mankind, may at a given time be better served by present violence than by evasion or submission. When, and how far, this is the case is a material question, depending on the existing situation and on the available possibilities of effective action. Morality dictates the broad principle that evil when used shall be used for good ends, combining insistence that it shall never be used except for good ends with due regard to the danger that by using it the good end may be forgotten, the good will be corrupted, or some better end defeated.[66]

But, of course, while war or the threat of war, the readiness to stand up and fight for what is right, may be necessary at times, war is still evil. It is evil because it makes power and not the procedure of reasoned discussion the means of decision. In repudiating the procedure of reasoned discourse wartime Japan, Nazi Germany and Fascist Italy left war as the only recourse for the preservation of democracy. Still in the end the principle of harmonious happiness must be extended to embrace all mankind. So long as the interests of the members of one state may impinge upon those of another there is conflict of interests. The problem is to resolve conflict, not by war or threat of war, not by diplomacy as an extension of war, but by the principle of harmonious happiness. Men must see that the good of the nation is a lesser good than the "greater good of all mankind," [67] by the principle of inclusiveness or universality.

In the present cold war there seems to be an impasse in the way of the development of the world polity. As Perry characterized things, Russia sees the ideal of democracy through the eye of social welfare. The United States tends to see it through the eye of the popular control of government. Both seem blind, only in different eyes, to the full ideal of democracy.[68] The impasse is not to be eliminated by the promulgation of the full ideal. It is doubtful whether anything can be done in a direct way to get Russia to open both eyes. Moreover, matters are not helped by pointing to the other fellow's blindness while ignoring one's own. One might best start by putting his own house in order.

So long as the United States is delinquent in living up to the full ideal of democracy internally and in its relations with the people of other nations, Russia may continue to see the United States as against the advancement of social welfare for its people and the people of the world. The ideological conflict between these two nations for the minds of mankind must become a conflict between the full ideal and the half-blind ideal. While there is no guarantee that Russia will change its view of the United States, the point is to give them no good reason for believing in it. Perry could not guarantee an end of conflict. He could try to describe how the world might operate best by co-operation. And he could describe the minimum requirements for the United States in contributing to the world co-operation as the commitment in deed as well as word to the full ideal of democracy for all people. And, success in attainment of this ideal required the commitment of all peoples to the inclusion of all peoples in the democratic community.

Let there be no mistake about Perry's position here. If a democratic world community was to exist it was to "be democratic in its parts." If it was to rest "on the agreement of nations" it must be remembered that "nations in the composite capacity can not agree—only persons can agree." [69] In sum, meaningful agreement of nations must rest upon the meaningful agreement of the persons whose interests are to be represented by their delegates to the community of nations.[70] While Perry's theory clearly allowed for differences among nations in particular patterns of values, he insisted that only one means for the determination of such patterns was justified.[71] On this point the thinking in all societies had to coincide if there was to be a world community. A world community had to be a community of nations organized internally on essentially democratic lines with appropriate procedures for the delegation and control of authority. The practical task for the ideology of democracy is to develop a universal allegiance to universal democracy.

Whether or not the goal of universal democracy will be achieved cannot be decided in advance. Whether men will be able to bring it off in practice no one can tell. One would not be justified, however, in bringing this uncertainty in evidence against Perry's theory of democracy. He did not pretend to predict the future. He painted a picture of what the future might be like and pointed out the hurdles to be overcome in constructing a world to conform to that painting. The tasks that he presented were not to be accomplished by presenting them. Perry sought the fundamental solution to these tasks in education. They provided him with the statement of the problem for the design of theory of education.

1. Ralph Barton Perry, *The Moral Economy* (New York: Charles Scribner's Sons, 1909); Ralph Barton Perry, *One World in the Making* (New York: Current Books, A. A. Wynn, 1945); Ralph Barton Perry, *The Citizen Decides: A Guide to Responsible Thinking in Time of Crisis* (Bloomington: Indiana University Press, 1951); and RV, especially p. vii. It is not vitally important to determine that Perry actually did set out initially in search of the best society. It is sufficient to note that this interpretation is not inconsistent with the content of his published works in their historical presentation. If the biographer objects that there is a difference between determining the actual intentions of a writer and making sense out of his writings by imputing intentions to him, it may be said in rebuttal that the purpose of the present discussion is to make sense out of Perry's position. The examination of Perry's theory of society is structured in accordance with this interpretation.

2. PD, pp. 47–50, cf. chap. xx and "Conclusion."

3. Ibid., pp. 19–23; RV, p. 272.

4. RV, p. 274.

5. GTV, p. 141.

6. RV, p. 137; Perry's quotes.

7. RV, p. 147.

8. Ibid., p. 148.

9. PD, pp. 359, 410–11, 434–36, and RV, pp. 65–66.

10. RV, pp. 137–39.

11. Ibid., p. 139.

12. Ibid., pp. 140–47.

13. Ibid., pp. 149–52.

14. Ibid., p. 150; Perry's italics.

15. Ibid., p. 153; Perry's italics.

16. Ibid., pp. 153–54; Perry's italics.

17. Ibid., chap. xi *passim*, see especially pp. 176–77.

18. Ibid., p. 123; Perry's italics.

19. Ibid., pp. 132–33; Perry's italics.

20. Ibid., pp. 132–36, see especially his notion of "empirical proof in the full sense," pp. 135–36.

21. Ibid., p. 181.

22. PD, pp. 572 and 579.

23. RV, p. 181; Perry's quotes.

24. Ibid., pp. 198, 214–15.

25. Ibid., p. 202.

26. Ibid., pp. 203–14.

27. Ibid., p. 215.

28. Ibid., p. 205.

29. PD, pp. 33–35.

30. Ralph Barton Perry, *Characteristically American*, The William Cook Foundation Lectures (New York: Alfred Knopf, 1949).

31. PD, pp. 48–61.

32. Ibid., pp. 89–90, 93–96, chap. ix and x, especially p. 242.

33. Ibid., p. 628.

34. Ibid., pp. 110–16.

35. Ibid., pp. 479–81.

36. Ibid., pp. 571–72, also see esp. RV, p. 214.

37. PD, p. 480.

38. Ibid., p. 481.

39. Ibid., p. 492.

40. Ibid., p. 630.

41. RV, chap. xiv passim.

42. PD, pp. 503–5; RV, chap. xiv, pp. 231 ff.

43. PD, pp. 572–75.

44. Ibid., p. 412.

45. Ibid., p. 405.

46. Ibid., p. 503.

47. RV, pp. 264–67, and PD, pp. 503–8.

48. PD, pp. 512 ff., and RV, pp. 285–86.

49. This is the argument of PD, chap. xviii and RV, pp. 288–89.

50. RV, p. 274.

51. Ibid.

52. Ibid., pp. 234–46, especially 245–46.

53. William James, *The Will to Believe and Other Essays in Popular Philosophy* (New York: Longmans, Green & Co., 1927).

54. RV, p. 273.

55. Ibid.

56. Ibid., p. 362.

57. Ibid., p. 304; Perry's italics.

58. Ibid., p. 309; Perry's italics.

59. Ibid.

60. Ibid., p. 276.

61. Ibid., p. 275; Perry's quotes and italics. It might be noted that here is one instance at least where Perry seems to admit the logical translatability of an affirmative into the negation of its polar opposite.

62. Ibid., pp. 275–76.

63. Ibid., pp. 314–22, 403–9.

64. Karl R. Popper, *The Open Society and Its Enemies* (Princeton: Princeton University Press, 1950), and RV, p. 405 n.

65. Popper, op. cit., p. 463; Popper's quotes.

66. RV, p. 220.

67. Ibid., p. 217.

68. Ibid., p. 281.

69. Ibid., pp. 294–95.

70. Ibid., p. 295.

71. Ibid., pp. 218–20, 288.

V. Perry's Theory of Education*

It would be rather naïve to suppose that education is the answer to all the problems of society. Education cannot guarantee to cure all social ills and to dissipate all evils. It would be equally naïve, however, to suppose that progress toward the realization of the ideal democracy, as Perry conceived it, could be made without attending to the question: 'What sort of education would be *best* as education for democracy?' At the very least one would want to determine whether certain

* The depth of Perry's concern for education for democracy is not to be measured by the number of his books which include 'education' in their titles. He wrote none. However, one cannot read very many of his books without appreciating Perry's recognition of the importance of this topic. GTV, see especially pp. 522–25, 681–82; PD, see especially pp. 192–93, 480, 495 and ff., and 573; Ralph Barton Perry, *One World in the Making* (New York: Current Books, A. A. Wynn, 1945), esp. chap. vii; Ralph Barton Perry, *The Citizen Decides: A Guide to Responsible Thinking in Time of Crisis* (Bloomington: Indi-University Press, 1951), esp. chap. v–vii; Ralph Barton Perry, *The Humanity of Man*, ed. Evelyn Ann Masi (New York: George Braziller, 1956), esp. chap. ii, "A Definition of the Humanities," and RV, chap. xxi. But Perry did not just write his theory of education. He was intimately connected with the development of the educational pattern at Harvard.

practices are detrimental to the development of democracy and this suggests that there are criteria or standards which education for democracy should try to meet. Perry's theory of education consisted in his elucidation and elaboration of such standards. The science of education, as he saw it, was the business of designing educational practices in accordance with these standards. And, so long as science must be an unfinished business, so long, that is, as the last words on thinking, knowing, learning and teaching remain to be written, there could be no guarantee of the success of the endeavor. Nevertheless, it is obvious that unless the endeavor is made there is no reason at all to support the supposition that democracy will develop in the direction of the ideal. The message of fairy tales to the contrary notwithstanding, 'wishing won't make it so.'

The Function of Education and Theory of Society

If Perry's theory of society was intended as an analysis of society to permit the construction of a theory of the best society, one might look for the parallel in his theory of education. The first step was to consider the role of education as a social institution. As Perry viewed things the question was 'What is the peculiar function of education as an institution of Society?' Another way of putting the question might be 'What social purposes are performed by education?' The next step involved the establishment of the principles of harmonious integration as the criteria for the evaluation of education for the best society. Here the question might have been 'By what principles is one to determine the proper sort of education for democracy?' Finally, these principles were applied to several views of education presumed appropriate to democracy and by this application these views were found wanting. As each of these steps is considered in turn it will appear that the parallel with his theory of society is not so clear cut as might have been expected.

Relation of education to society.—Perry summarized his view of the over-arching purpose of education in the following:

> In the fundamental sense education is the cultural process by which successive generations of men take their places in history. Nature has assigned an indispensable role to education through the prolongation of human infancy, and through the plasticity of human faculties. By nature man is not equipped for life but with capacities that enable him to learn how to live. Since it is generally agreed that acquired characteristics are not inherited education assumes the full burden of bringing men "up to date," creating "the modern man" of the . . . latest model. Through education men acquire the civilization of the past, and are enabled both to take part in the civilization of the present, and make the civilization of the future. In short, the purpose of education is threefold: inheritance, participation, and contribution.[1]

There is a peculiarity in this hypostatization of "nature" and of "education" that is not easily explained away as merely an expression of literary style. As one may recall Perry himself had insisted upon the careful examination of instances of the personification or reification of 'society' or 'social force.' What importance can be attached to his apparent personification, not so much of nature but, of education?

The question here is whether it makes any sense to talk about education's having a purpose. If Perry wanted to be consistent he should have spoken more directly of the purposes which people have for education, for on his view only persons have purposes. In fact, Perry was stipulating an overview of the purpose of education. He was not stating what this purpose had to be. He was stating what it had to be if there was to be any communication between his theory of education and his theory of society.

On the whole he seems to have favored a balanced view of education. He would not allow the claims for exclusiveness of purpose of the respective proponents of inheritance, participa tion or contribution. In effect, he was saying that education ought not to be viewed as a "mere deposit and preservation of the past"; it ought not to be taken as the "mere fitting of individuals to an existing society"; it ought not to be looked upon "as a mere preparation for the years to come, whether in this world or the next." [2] But, then why should education not be viewed as any one of these to the exclusion of the others? As will be seen further on Perry actually did subordinate the first two of these to the third.

Perry's argument for this balanced view began simply enough. First of all given the nature of man, the fact that he brings with him at birth only the capacity to learn to sustain himself on earth, it is clear that inheritance is an important aspect of education. Were it not for man's ability to transmit what he has learned to succeeding generations "each genera- tion would be compelled to begin the life of man all over again." [3] Clearly there is this minimum requirement for edu- cation that it should enable man to sustain his life as man. And now, although Perry did not put things in *quite* so simple terms, it should be clear that an education based on the inheritance of enough knowledge to maintain existence is an education for participation in the present for recipients of that education. Moreover, it is for them intended also as an educa- tion for the future, to prepare them to continue to exist when their education is over.

Of course, Perry did not put matters so simply and one might hazard a guess as to why he did not. If the purpose of education is taken as the provision of the bare minimum to insure that human life does not have to begin anew in each generation, then no reasonable distinctions can be made among education for inheritance, participation and preparation for future life. Man could go on teaching his young to sharpen sticks and dig for roots forever secure in his knowledge that he would be educating in accordance with the threefold purpose of education. In this light not only are arguments over which of these three is the true purpose of education foolish, but it seems trivial to point it out. Nor, does it seem particularly edifying in this simplified model to point out that education is both personal and social.[4] In this 'primitive' society, the well-being of the person and of the society are most intimately bound together in the purpose of education. The purpose of education is the survival of society through the survival of its members.

However, when one turns to the mainstreams of life in what might be called twentieth-century western civilization, matters appear in a different light. There is considerably more to be inherited than stick-sharpening and root-digging. The fact that men have not always been content to see the future as the past continued, leaves the so-called modern man with the problem of selecting from his inheritance that which might serve him in good stead in fitting himself to an exceedingly complex present. Included in his inheritance are forces, not forces in some mysterious sense but as activities of men, which affect his life in the present in myriad ways and which make his present but a succession of pauses in the rush to an unpredictable future. It was in this context that Perry spoke of the three-fold purpose of education. And in so doing Perry was evaluating education by the standards of the ideal society.

Harmonious integration as the criterion.—In conceiving education as a science Perry took it as concerned with three basic questions: "What are the conditions and forces which bring education to pass? Is it good or bad education? What are the methods by which an educational end can be realized?" [5] Perry's elucidation of the third question exemplified the impact intended by his conception of education as a science:

> Educational science has . . . its technology. Given any task which involves the shaping of men's minds, educational science will tell him [*sic*] how to do it. . . . Education for war and conquest and education for peace and freedom draw from the same bag of tricks. In short educational technology, like all technology, is neutral. The range of educational technology is as wide as the range of causes and conditions, mental and physical, which produce educational effects.[6]

It appears that educational views are to be evaluated by the standard of the intention to educate no matter what purpose is taken for education. This suggestion of technological neutrality was supported in Perry's further elaboration of the range of the first question. As he saw it, it calls for an explanation of the content of the curriculum and the manner of transmitting that content in any particular society in the light of the historical traditions and dominant interests of that society. It calls for the explanation of the educational system itself in relation to the history of the forces and attitudes which shaped its development.[7] One need not judge the merits of these interests and attitudes in pointing them out as influences.

However, one might want to make such judgments. This was the role of educational science as included in the expanded view of the second question 'is it good or bad education?':

> The existing educational practices may be judged by the prejudices of the judge or his class; by the prevailing conscience of the times; by political, legal, or economic standards, by aesthetic or scientific interests or scruples; by the articles of a religious faith or an ideal of piety; by the general characteristics of a social or national culture. Of such external critiques there is no end. Suffice it here to recognize the legitimacy of all such critiques, in order to pass on to the internal critique, that is, the judgment of education by what education is for.[8]

Perry's distinction here between the internal and external normative critiques was either misleading or confused. The issue is not so much the legitimacy of evaluation of education by such external criteria. Certainly, people can and will make such evaluations. Of course, whether it is proper to view them as legitimate practices of the educational scientist *qua* scientist in deciding what is good or bad education is debatable. However, in focusing upon the internal critique Perry short-circuited any such debate.

In effect, he asserted the legitimacy of certain of these practices of the educational scientist by incorporating particular external criteria in his internal criteria in a rather confusing manner. Nevertheless, it was an important confusion for his theory of education. His position was as follows:

> The ulterior purpose of education . . . extends beyond morality. Education is concerned not only to harmonize

the individual's several interests and fit him for participation in a peaceful and coöperative social life, but to develop his intellectual and aesthetic interests for their own sakes and advance him as far as possible toward their own intrinsic perfections.[9]

Now all sorts of questions might suggest themselves. But one stands out above the others as the crucial question. It is not so important to ask here whether these intellectual and aesthetic interests are really inherent in individuals. The important question is why they should be developed toward whatever Perry meant by "their own intrinsic perfections."

Perry's use of the word 'ulterior' here suggests that the fostering of this development is a defining characteristic of education. But, people may claim to see different defining characteristics of education or may take this characteristic to mean something other than that which Perry intended. Thus, for example, some might claim that the ulterior purpose of education is to encourage the quest for truth and beauty as defined and certified by church or party. Human beings may be rather easily satisfied in their quests for answers in the search for truth and beauty and perhaps they are not so much concerned with the quest as with the possession of answers that satisfy them. Why should it not be the business of education to give them the sort of answers that would stop them from seeking further? The fact that this has not always been possible should no more stand in the way of such an attempt than the fact that democracy has not always been able to sustain itself should stand in the way of the attempt to make it work. One must be careful not to confuse 'the purposes for which education might be used' with 'purposes of education.' The notion of 'ulterior purpose' implies that justification of a particular purpose is not called for; if one is going to educate, he must accept this ulterior purpose. So long as conflicting interpretations of ulterior purpose are conceivable, a discussion of the 'purposes of education' would not be particularly helpful in resolving the conflicts. If an institution is to be judged in terms of its rationale, then education must be discussed in terms of the purposes which people intend it to serve. And, this raises the question of the justification of Perry's conception of the so-called ulterior purpose of education.

Its justification lay in its inclusion in Perry's theory of the ideal democracy. It was presumed as a central conception in the principle of harmonious happiness as it was developed in Perry's theory of value into the standard of highest value in the meaning of morality. Perry's remarks on moral education are instructive on this point:

> When morality is . . . conceived as the form of personal and social organization which gives to individuals and minority groups the maximum of freedom consistent with living together peacefully and fruitfully; when it is conceived as fulfillment and not as negation of life; when it encourages diverse spontaneities and aspirations, requiring only that they shall not violate one another, and thus promises to the arts and sciences the fullest opportunity, consistently with order, to follow their own inherent passions for beauty and truth—when in short it *makes room* and does not merely confine, or confines only in order to make room—then it is seen to coincide with precisely those high motives which have led men to suspect moral education.[10]

Again, it is not so important whether these passions for beauty and truth are inherent so long as it is realized that Perry's view of morality took them as such. It was his view of morality that required his conception of them as inherent and as the ulterior purpose of education. His principle of harmonious integration was the ultimate criterion for the definition and evaluation of education.

Other views of education for democracy considered.—In setting forth the three-fold purpose of education as "inheritance, participation, and contribution" Perry was insisting upon the impossibility of conceiving the present as static, the future as a continuing changeless past. To those who might concentrate on education for inheritance he said, in effect, 'But look, we cannot live yesterday; we must live today.' Or, in his own words, "Those who inherit the civilization of the past must *live it in their own day*; hence there can be no separation between education as inheritance and education as participation." [11] Still, what answer could he give to those who might insist that it is better to return to the ways of the past than to proceed in the mad dash to the future? To those who would concentrate on education for participation in the present he could say, in effect, that the present is always a prelude to the future, as a set of partially completed tasks suggesting always something to be desired for their completion.[12] Still, what answer could he give to those who might insist that what *is* now is good enough; that man has come a long way from his early beginnings and that it would be vain and dangerous to let him go further? Finally, to those who would emphasize education for the future Perry could say, in effect, that the very unpredictability of the future makes education for the future meaningless unless it is grounded in the ideas, sentiments, and habits—the knowledge and the standards—which have come from the past.[13] Still, what answer could he give to those who might insist that it is the purpose of education to assist youth in the creation of knowledge and of their own standards for the continuing development of a new society; that only the last word is important and not the first; that one must move as quickly as possible from the most recent knowledge to the development of new knowledge? After all, which habits of the past would one pass on, those of laziness or avarice? What knowledge would one pass on, the geocentric picture of the universe? What values would one pass on, those of a Caligula or a Hitler?

All of these questions raise the issue of the meaningfulness of Perry's insistence on the three-fold purpose of education. They show that there is nothing in the notions of education or society that requires the acceptance of all these purposes. There is a common strain running through these questions either implicitly or explicitly. They all involve questions of value. They all raise the issue of what would be best for man and for society. Perry's conception of the purpose of education assumed meaning as it spoke to such questions. It presumed his theory of value and theory of the ideal society as its support.

But wait, is it necessary to go to Perry's theory of the ideal society for the answer to these questions? It might be pointed out that, after all, it would be unrealistic to ignore any of these elements in education. Thus, for example, one might insist that whether one likes it or not he cannot expect to hide in the past from factors already set in motion that will have bearing on his future. Just because man is born *in medias res* his attempts to return to the past or maintain the present as static must be frustrated. The answers of the past to the problems of existence in the past cannot be applied directly and in the same ways to the problems of existence in the present. For, the problems of the present are not the same as those of the past.

Unfortunately there are two difficulties in this position. First, it is not inconceivable that man's inability to solve a most urgent problem in the present may lead to the destruction of the great fabric of civilization. This could mean the return to the barest forms of social organization to maintain the existence of those if any who might survive the holocaust of atomic warfare. If this would not be a return to the past then it is surely the nearest thing to it. And in the second place, while it might be unlikely it is not inconceivable that enough men might band together in a sort of mass reaction and turn their backs on the contemporary world. As the problems of the present become increasingly complex, as the future becomes increasingly unpredictable due to present complexity, the comparative certainty and order of an age gone by may become increasingly desirable. The man on the white horse who promises a return to that certainty and order might not have to seek too hard for followers. By what standards would such men be unreasonable in thus conceiving the ideal future as a return to the past?

For Perry, it is clear, they would be unreasonable by the standard of harmonious happiness. To return to the past is to throw out the good with the bad or else it is not a return. To return to the past is to settle for a limited integration of interests. It is to deny the quest for the increasing maximization of good. It is to deny the possibility of human progress through human effort toward the realization of ever-expanding possibilities for human well-being. It is to settle for less than one might have. Perry's position was clearly expressed in the following:

> Democratic education is . . . a peculiarly ambitious education. It does not educate men for prescribed places in life, shaping them to fit the requirements of a preëxisting and rigid division of labor. Its idea is that the

social system itself, which determines what places there are to fill, shall be created by the men who fill them. It is true that in order to live and to live effectively men must be adapted to their social environment, but only that they may in the long run adapt the environment to themselves. Men are not building materials to be fitted to a preëstablished order, but are themselves the architects of order.[14]

To return to the past or to attempt to fix the present is to assume that there is a social order to which men must conform. But to focus on the future is not to ignore the past or present. Nor is it to attempt to pass on all the habits, ideas and attitudes of the past or to select from the past only those habits, ideas, and attitudes to be passed on to those who are to be educated. For "education for democracy implies the development of a capacity of personal self-determination." [15] The individual student must learn his own lessons; his teachers cannot learn them for him. However, his teachers must help him to learn those lessons which will help him to play his role in the shaping of a progressively democratic society. This was **Perry's** message in his view of liberal education.

Liberal Education

If Perry's conception of liberal education were summed up in slogan form it might appear as 'Liberal education for liberation of man.' Fortunately, Perry's views were sufficiently detailed so that their examination does not entail mere exegesis from such a slogan. Still, it does point up the breadth of his conception of liberal education. As he put it, "liberal education teaches men to enjoy and exercise their freedom, and to spread and extend its domain." [16]

The concept of liberation.—Those who profess their faith in liberal education might do well to look closely at the nature of the responsibility that they have accepted. They can not, as Perry pointed out, assume that the individual might be left to develop his potentialities as he will. There is no reason to believe that he will turn out for the better rather than for the worse. "The standard of development is no standard at all unless some idea of *what is to be developed* is introduced or read between the lines." [17] Nor, can one assume that the minds of men are to be liberated if they are not given the opportunity of "exercising themselves, by following their interests, by trying to succeed . . . if education is to educate it must release the springs of such activities." [18] The liberal educator was reminded of his responsibilities in the following:

> It is one of the immense advantages of human over animal learning that a man can learn "cognitively," that is, from what other people have already learned, and not only from his own experience. If the human mind is to realize its greatest possibilities of growth, it must be nourished from without, if its activities are not to be random and wasteful, it must be guided; if it is to find what it needs, it must be told where to look; if it is to know, it must be compelled to face the stubborn facts of nature; if it is to learn how to live, it must adapt itself to its existing social environment. Education involves restraint, redirection and control, by those who "know better." Spontaneity and discipline are two halves of one whole, and they should not be separated by an either-or and developed into opposing educational cults.[19]

Liberal education was conceived by Perry as an education suitable to a free man, one whose life was to be "governed by his own choice." Accordingly, it was "to cultivate the art of choice and to provide it [choice] with eligible alternatives." Occupational education may be liberal to the extent that it has been preceded by an education which has prepared the individual to choose his occupation from a range of live options. Liberal education is opposed to dogmatic education which would have the individual's "mind made up *for him* rather than *by him.*" An education intended to impart a knowledge of facts is less liberal than that intended to impart a knowledge of principles, for "he who grasps the principles can then apply and extend them for himself." [20] Specialized education of any sort may be liberal or illiberal to the extent that it does or does not conduce to openness of mind. In the acquisition of a special form of expertness the opportunities may or may not be taken to bring together the principles gained elsewhere with this expertness and to develop new insights and keener understanding for the benefit of one's self and of society.[21]

The so-called humanities do not define a necessarily liberating body of studies, nor does the liberal arts college stand for a necessarily liberalizing institution of education. The idea of liberal or humanistic education is not to be confused with such mechanisms for the organization of the curriculum. "If the meaning of liberal education is to be understood, it must not be identified by labels or associated exclusively with any part of a university. Liberality is a norm or standard by which to judge educational practices wherever they occur." [22]

It appears, then, that it is the responsibility of those who would promote liberal education to do more than profess the merits of their ends. They must be prepared to indicate and justify by this standard what shall be taught. They must be on guard lest the manner in which it is taught should corrupt the liberalizing influence of what is taught. They must face these problems implicit in the practice of liberation.

The practice of liberation.—Perry did not just present the challenge. He was willing to face it. And, while he did not present a plan detailed in all respects for the content and methods of education from the first grade to the last postgraduate year, he did have a few observations to make on these topics. His remarks were most specifically relevant to the level of college education. This is, of course, quite understandable, for this was the level with which he was most familiar as a practitioner, both as a teacher and as one who was engaged in the continuing business of curriculum design and the development of educational policy.

Perry would allow no sharp dividing lines between elementary and secondary education. He could see elementary education not as "a finished product, complete in itself, but as a phase of unfolding." Elementary education could not be viewed merely as the "teaching and learning of 'the elements,' such as the 'three R's.' " [23] Human beings do not move from childhood to adolescence to maturity in clear and discrete steps so that one could easily mark the length of time in elementary or secondary school. If the child is viewed as a growing adult, "his education must not only feed his growth but stimulate it, and offer the individual something which lies at the ever-widening circumference of his existing powers." [24] The liberation of the mind must start early and not after a number of years of schooling intended to prepare for a liberal education which will begin later. It is the individual mind that is to be liberated and therefore requires furnishing and stimulation as it is ready and in order to help it to become ready for increased furnishing and stimulation. This does not mean that the child must be viewed only as an adult in the making; "he is a person. . . . He has his world to live in; and he must live in the same world with his contemporary elders." [25]

If over-emphasis upon the rigid distinction between elementary education and the rest of liberal education was an unhealthy abstraction, according to Perry, so too was early emphasis upon vocational education. While the individual must at some time acquire marketable skills he is not somehow designed for a particular occupation. "To educate him only for a division of labor is to mutilate him." The job of education is "to educate a *man* and not a mere interchangeable part of the social mechanism." [26] Perry was insistent on this point:

> It is contrary to the principle of democracy that its members should be sorted out at an early age and prepared for occupations for which there is a social demand. It matters not whether this distinction is made by aptitude tests, or by the numerical limitations of educational opportunity—if careers are assigned to men before they have reached the stage of maturity and enlightenment at which they can decide for themselves society has failed to equip them for the role of sovereignty to which, in a democracy, they are called.[27]

It is sufficient to note at this juncture that Perry's criticism of overemphasis upon vocational education stems in part from his concern for the liberation of the individual mind as a prior condition to occupational choice. This point will be discussed further in a later section as it relates to the problem of equality of educational opportunity. But, now it is time to discuss Perry's views on the content of secondary and higher education. Perry set the stage for the discussion in the following admonition:

> If the curriculum is to be judged by its purpose of education the admission of any subject matter must be tested by the lesson to be learned. How far, and in what respects, does it put the learner in possession of his cultural inheritance, enable him to participate in the contemporary world, and qualify him to contribute to the civilization of the future? [28]

From natural science the student should learn that "his lot is cast in a physical environment, by which he is controlled, and which he can control in turn." He should learn the meaning of truth and acquire a respect for its objectivity. He should also acquire the spirit of inquiry and at the same time "learn the limits of science, and its role for better or worse, in civilization." [29]

From the social sciences he should also learn "similar lessons of objectivity, rigorous thought, and intellectual invention." [30] But he must learn much more than this. The difference between the culture which man makes and the nature which he finds must be emphasized. He must know where he comes from in order to shape the society that he is to make. He must view the lessons of history and sociology both as lessons to orient him to the present and, by the application of moral criteria, as the definitions of his tasks in the proper shaping of future society. "He should learn the perspective and the patience which are required for all long-range human achievements; and courage to face the indeterminate future." [31]

From literature and the fine arts he should learn the meaning and excitement of aesthetic enjoyment. He should develop taste and discrimination. He should feel some impulsion toward creativity. Above all, he should acquire "a love of truth and beauty as ends in themselves which transcend the utilities of practical life and the bare requirements of morality." [32]

From philosophy "whether it be taught under that name by so called philosophers or conveyed through the philosophical-mindedness of teachers of other subjects" he should learn to appreciate the inclusiveness of things. And, "philosophy should stimulate the critical faculties and" lead him to "challenge every ready-made assumption." Stemming from his study of philosophy he should be set in the path of a faith to live by. And, "from the study of religion and of education itself, the individual should learn of those values which not only embrace the requirements of man's organized living but add some glimpse of perfection." [33]

The above was not intended as a practicable program of study. According to Perry it was designed "only to provide criteria by which from a vast range of subject matter formal education shall select, within the limits of time and capacity, that which will best serve the purpose of an education for all." [34] It was not intended to imply the exclusion from the curriculum of the learning of specific skills or information or the development of specialized competence in particular areas. However, it should be obvious that it was intended to produce considerably more than a specialist or a well-rounded gentleman.

This selection of the content of the curiculum emphasized the moral purpose of education as Perry saw it. Perry did not say, for example, that one must learn history, but that one must learn certain lessons from history. It required not just teachers but teacher-scholars, for how else could one "learn what knowledge is, and how it is advanced" except from "one who practices what he preaches and exhibits the methods and passion of inquiry in his own person." [35] It required the establishment through literature and the arts of such a love of truth and beauty as to lead the individual to view them as transcending the "utilities of practical life and the bare requirements of morality." [36] And, as has been seen, it was quite important to Perry's theory of morality that individuals should thus view truth and beauty. In its emphasis on the teaching of philosophy for imparting the view of the inclusiveness of the universe it was in effect paving the way for the faith in man's capacity to shape his world in accordance with the principles of inclusiveness as set forth in Perry's conception of harmonious integration. It was a selection based on the educational requirements of an organized attempt at insuring commitment to the development of the ideal democracy.

The Problem of Commitment to Democracy

If the individual may develop his potential for good as well as for evil it was to be the job of education to make sure that it would be developed for good. Perry spoke of a "democracy which educates for democracy." [37] He saw education as "not merely a boon conferred by democracy but as a condition of its survival and of its becoming that which it undertakes to be." [38] But to foster such an end education for democracy was to do more than to spread enlightenment; it was to foster the individual's commitment to the proper use of his enlightenment. The problem of education for democracy was, first, to face the need for commitment and, then, to accept the responsibility for the attempt to ensure it.

The need for the insurance of commitment.—It may seem trite to say it but it is nonetheless true that an increase in the ability of man to control his environment may contribute equally as well to man's humanity or to his inhumanity to his fellow man. The fire may warm the invited guest or burn down the house of a hated competitor. Considering the advantage to be gained for all people in the extension of knowledge to all people one would hardly want to stop this extension by a one-sided view which concentrates solely upon its possible disadvantages. If democracy requires the intellectual levelling up of all its citizens then it must speak to the consequences of the extension of knowledge. Perry put the problem as follows:

> Democracy is that form of social organization which most depends on personal character and moral autonomy. The members of a democratic society cannot be the wards of their betters; for there is no class of betters but only a better part gathered from all the members, and finding collective expression in what is called "public opinion." This, which in a democracy is the ultimate authority, is not, strictly speaking, opinion, but an interested attitude, a being for or against, a will, which is to be judged by moral standards as good will or ill will, and by cognitive standards as mediated by truth or error. The cultivation and firm implanting of enlightened good will in the body of its citizens is, then, the fundamental task of education for citizenship in a democracy.[39]

The problem, then, was to insure that enlightenment served good will or that it was colored by good will. It was to insure that if enlightenment was to serve a prejudice it was to serve the right prejudice, the moral prejudice. "Morality," according to Perry, "*is* a prejudice—a prejudice in favor of justice and benevolence." [40] But, then this raises a peculiar problem.

If by prejudice one implies a prejudgment of an issue, a commitment to a position prior to its examination or without benefit of examination, is it not odd to mash it together with enlightenment in the concept of 'enlightened good will'? How can one claim that morality as Perry conceived it is a prejudice and at the very same time insist that it "appeal to reason"? [41] This is confusing. As he took moral education to be an extremely important ingredient in education for democracy, a closer look at his position here is called for.

Perry recognized that moral education must be geared to the level of educability of the individual. The lowest form of moral education was to proceed by the imposition of sanctions, either punishments applied directly or those of the "accusing consciences of others." There was also moral education through initiation into "the partial or prudential meaning of morality— through recognition of its so-called 'natural consequences' for himself." The last stage involved "acquiring a good will" by appeal "to reason, this being taken to mean men's faculty for objectivity . . . to see themselves as others see them and others as these others see themselves"; and by appeal to "that natural sympathy . . . or fellow-feeling which moves one individual to adopt another's interest, and be moved to its support." [42]

If one looks closely he will find that success in the highest stage depends upon the success of moral education at the lowest level to cause the individual to color his prudence so that he takes 'objectivity' as Perry defined it. Moreover, to appeal to natural sympathy as he defined it was to beg the question. The problem of insuring good will was the problem of insuring this 'natural sympathy.'

It would appear that Perry feared a prudential approach to morality as conducing to selfishness, which, by his definition, would have been a denial of morality. In spite of the dangers attending the creation of a cult of selfishness, it is not at all clear that Perry's view of morality and of the right to indoctrinate that view could not be established from prudence as a basic principle. Perry's arguments for indoctrination seem to suggest this possibility.

Indoctrination for democracy—imposition vs. influence.— Perry advocated indoctrination for democracy. He identified doctrines of democracy and proposed that they be indoctrinated. It would be rather unfair, however, to condemn his position on the presumption that indoctrination is necessarily incompatible with the very ideals or doctrines of democracy. As will be seen one must consider what is to be indoctrinated *and* how it is to be indoctrinated.

Perry considered as absurd the charge that education for specific preconceived ends would be too purposeful. Granted that totalitarian societies promoted indoctrination for unquestioning allegiance to the expressed will of the dictator. In such societies the pattern of education is certainly purposeful in "the harnessing of every available force that will contribute to the result [intended], and [in] the relentless exclusion of every distracting or opposing influence." [43] Not that success in indoctrination can be guaranteed, but the extent of the success of indoctrination in totalitarian societies is worth noting, and, also worth noting is the fact that it reflects the care involved in the translation of educational ends into educational practice. Still, is not success similarly the goal of education for democracy? Perry characterized the apparent dilemma of education for democracy as follows:

To define in advance an end result and then to seek by all possible means to achieve it, is held to be too narrowing, too repressive, too authoritarian. But if, on the other hand, there is no end in view, educational activity is confused and incoherent. Its various parts and successive phases do not add up to anything. Without a definition of the end there is no test by which means can be selected, and no standard by which practice can be criticized and improved.[44]

But there is a way out of this apparent dilemma, for in fact, it is not a dilemma at all. If one objects to the narrowness, rigidity and authoritarianism of indoctrination for totalitarianism "he must be *for* their opposites: namely breadth, flexibility, and freedom."[45] The possible means for the indoctrination of these ends do not involve the imposition of beliefs which are not to be questioned or a daily recitation of a catechism of democracy. Just because totalitarianism strives for success in educating for totalitarianism, democracy is not therefore to hamstring itself from indoctrinating democracy. For, the means for the indoctrination of democracy, 'all possible means,' are not in all respects the same as those for the indoctrination of totalitarianism. And, the propriety of these means to do the job is determined by the nature of the job to be done:

To enable the student to think for himself and make up his own mind; to implant in him a respect for the similar right and opportunity of others; to support institutions in which teachers and students shall enjoy intellectual and cultural freedoms among themselves; to create a society in which such institutions shall be promoted and pro- tected, and which shall be pervaded throughout by similar freedoms—this is a positive end, than which no end could be more positive and constructive. It defines a task calling for devotion, courage, and effort. It is capable of creating its symbols, saints, heroes, and martyrs.[46]

It defines indoctrination for democracy as the task of ensuring openness and freedom not by the imposition of meaningless maxims or by controlling thought, but by helping to free thought, subject only to the requirement that all individuals are to become thus freed. The advocate of democracy cannot consistently object to the influence of the teacher in imparting his own scholarly integrity. For, "he who opposes such indoctrination will himself exemplify it." [47]

Implicit in this view is the modeling of the democratic society on the academic community of scholars. As Perry stated "the rightful freedom of minds, the maxims of consistency and experimental proof, of intellectual honesty, of tolerance and persuasion are themselves doctrines." [48] These are beliefs and conditions necessary to the advancement of knowledge and to the exercise of intellectual freedom. It suggests the possibility that it is in the best interests of all thinking individuals to contribute to the creation of that society which will permit them to think. This suggestion will be examined in further detail in the concluding chapter. But, first there are a few implications for education stemming from Perry's views of value and society yet to be brought out.

Further Implications of Perry's Theory of Value
and Theory of Society for Education

In developing his theory of education as education for democracy Perry sought to outline a view of education consistent with his theory of value and theory of society. But he sought more than consistency of theory; he proposed a theory of education designed to establish the primacy of his theories of value and of society in the minds of men. There are three major implications for education stemming from this effort which may have been suggested in what has preceded but which are worth bringing to the fore. The first is that there can be no argument from the right to ignorance against the duty of democracy to educate all people for democracy. The second is that education for democracy must face the problem of the control of informal as well as formal education. And the third is that education for democracy presumes acceptance of the risks in free inquiry. Each of these implications is discussed in turn.

The notion of equality and equality of educational opportunity.—If the ultimate in the realization of the ideal of democracy lies in the universality of the extension of democracy, it is not enough to extend the benefits of education for democracy to a limited group of people. Education for democracy, according to Perry, must be universal. Perry pinned his hopes for world order not just on the creation of world mindedness in the citizens of one country or among one group of citizens of one country, but on his "faith in the educability and reeducability of all men and nations." [49]

If democracy requires education for democracy whether for national or international democracy, then, it must face the problem of overcoming the hesitancy or objections of those who would not have their young thus educated. The problem here is not the extremely important practical problem of coercion or persuasion. Undoubtedly, both would be necessary, but conjectures about how they may best be carried out lie primarily in the province of the political tactician. More important here is the consideration of the reasons why they would be necessary.

The obvious reasons are that one cannot argue with those who are incapable of reasonable argument or those who, though capable, are not willing to take the argument far enough, but instead introduce a premise that stops debate. To try to convince a savage by reasonable argument that he ought to educate his children to think for themselves just may not be practicable. To try to convince a laborer that he ought to put his son in the college course in high school may not be practicable if he cannot conceive of his son as bright enough to go to college or if he cannot see the advantages of a college education. One cannot argue with ignorance or anti-intellectualism. At the same time one cannot argue with those who fall back on an article of social or religious dogma and refuse to carry on the argument. Those who would refuse to educate the negro because they claim to know that he is inherently inferior to the white and yet will not submit their knowledge claim to test cannot be reasoned with. Those who insist that it is against the doctrines of their religion to permit the discussion of religion (not the inculcation of religion) in the public schools may be quite reasonable on other issues but not on that one.

The most subtle argument stopper is the one that presumes to speak in the name of democracy. This is the argument that it is contrary to the principle of individual or parental choice to tamper with an individual and to influence him so that he starts questioning the assumptions of his parents or his religion, so that he starts thinking for himself. 'Who has the right,' it might be asked, 'to alienate the child from his family or subcultural group?'

But this is a curious sort of line to take. It only seems to be grounded in the rights of the individual. The question may be asked, 'Are these the individual's right to remain ignorant and his right to choose, say, his path in education or his path toward an occupation, on the basis of a limited, rather than his widest possible apprehension of his potentialities and his alternatives?' How does one defend the right to ignorance? To say, for example, that ignorance is bliss is to say no more than that a man is happy when he thinks he is happy. One can still ask whether he is as happy as he might be if he knew enough to choose a different course from the one he has taken. To argue that he might risk unhappiness in extending himself toward the limits of his capacities will not work either. For by his very ignorance he is at the mercy of outside influences upon his happiness with less chance to control these influences than he would have if he were not so ignorant. To argue that man has the right to be happy with his lot whatever it may be and no matter what may befall him, is to argue that whatever *is* is good, that whatever happens ought to happen and that man ought to be happy whatever his lot. In answer to this, one might simply remark that, if this is the case, he ought to be happy to be educated— that this, then, is to be part of his lot.

But, what about the notion that it is undemocratic to alienate the child from the parent or the subculture by helping him to develop his capacity to think for himself? On what principles are these rights of the parent or the subculture over the child established? Do these influences speak in the name of individualism for the child or in the name of the right to insure their dominance over him? Do they not speak in the name of dogmatism rather than individualism? Are they not saying that the child has only the right to believe what he is told to believe or what he is permitted by others to believe, but not the right to question these beliefs? Surely, this is an odd sort of individualism that denies the child the full right to be an individual. In the end, if it is even to attempt to make sense, it must boil down to some form of the argument for the right of the individual to be ignorant.

Equal opportunity for education, then, is not to be barred by the argument from the right to ignorance. But in this discussion a problem has been raised of grave consequence to education for democracy. What is to be done to prevent people from advancing such arguments? This is the problem of the control of informal education.

Informal and formal education.—According to Perry "informal education is the greater part of education. It precedes, accompanies, permeates and supersedes formal education. Formal education is largely forgotten, and it is a part of its task to teach men to teach themselves and how to learn from influences which are not expressly designed for educational purposes." [50] But formal education was to do more than this; it was to teach men to control the agencies of informal education so that they might perform their functions in accordance with the purpose of education for democracy.

It is not possible in this limited space to speak on all the agencies of informal education. To discuss in any meaningful detail the influence of parents, peers, and play in and out of school at all ages and stages of life, as well as the influence of relatives, business associates, co-workers and the experiences gained in work or business on the shaping of attitudes and beliefs would require more than a section of a chapter on education. Or, as Perry put it, "to canvass the influences which impinge upon the individual throughout his life, which shape and mold his mind, would far exceed the limits of a mere chapter on education." [51] However, he did consider a most important influence of informal education—the influence of the instruments of mass communication.

Increasing literacy and increasing accessibility to the human mind of the agencies of mass communication with advancing technological sophistication are not in themselves good. This "multiplication of the instruments of education" may be *"for better or for worse."* These instruments may or may not serve the purpose of education for democracy. They may even serve to defeat the purpose of such education. Perry went so far as to say that "this, in large measure, is precisely what they do." [52]

Now, if education for democracy is to be directed toward certain sorts of purposes and not others, if informal education is viewed as by far the greatest part of education, and if the agencies of mass communication are an important part of informal education, then some means for the control of these agencies is required. Perry considered three alternatives for control and rejected the first two. "The first possibility is to reform the producers," by appealing to the individual producer's "sense of his educational responsibilities." This was rejected on the grounds that his economic interests in the necessity to compete to stay in business with those who might not have such a sense of responsibility may "operate as stronger incentives than his educational conscience." [53] An individual producer may have to decide *between* staying in business at all and meeting his educational responsibilities. "The second possibility is to place the agencies of mass communication under the control of the government, acting in the interest of public education." This was rejected on the grounds that this would give to the government the power to "create the opinion on which it rests, which violates the maxim that political authority rests with the people." [54] This is an odd objection if, in fact, the government takes Perry's view that education for democracy is an education to insure that authority rests with the people. For, then, it would appear to be the job of governmental educational control to insure that the people are aware of alternatives, and of their rights and duties to consider alternatives. However, there is the *danger*, but not the necessity as Perry seemed to think, that such power of control once concentrated in the hands of the government may be corrupted and misused so that the government assumes "the role of a colossal demagogue who treats the people as wards to be spoon-fed by their betters." [55] Perry rejected these possibilities in favor of the third.

The third possibility involved a less direct means of control. Rather than trying to remake the producers or to let the government remake the producers by acting as watchdog or censor, the solution, for Perry, lay in the reformation of the taste of the consumer through formal education. Now, it should be noted that Perry did not propose that all people, whatever their ages, be sent back to school to learn to choose what they should read or watch on television. Instead, he proposed "that during the period of his education proper [formal] the individual shall be made ready for his education improper [informal]. The phrase 'education to prepare for later life,' will be amended to add 'education to prepare for the education of later life.' " [56] Hopefully, formal education was to make the individual aware of the forces of education impinging upon him, and to increase his discriminatory ability to evaluate and make use of those forces for his own well-being and that of society. As Perry put it, education must help him to "acquire a sales resistance, and yet know how to buy; an initial skepticism which will nevertheless permit him to believe." [57]

This statement introduces another implication of Perry's views for education. It centers upon the tension between skepticism and the necessity for the acceptance of belief.

The problem of risk in the freedom of inquiry.—It is impossible to doubt everything all the time. If man is to maintain his existence he must believe, whether or not he verbalizes this belief, that he has an existence to maintain. At the moment that he eats a morsel of food he must believe in the existence of food by the fact of his eating even if he were to say 'All is an illusion including my eating.' For, he is playing the game, whether or not he says it is an illusion. The more serious questions for the individual are, 'What should I believe and what should I doubt?' The problem for education is to help prepare the individual to answer these questions. And, he must answer them within the limitations of his own capabilities:

> There are vast bodies of attested truth, within the domain of the natural and social sciences which may properly be accepted on authority, since their proof lies beyond the capacity or the leisure of the layman. Only a minute portion of mankind can understand the evidence for nuclear physics, or the theory of relativity, or the principles of heredity, or the chemical composition of celestial bodies, or the historical causes of the French Revolution. If the educated man's beliefs were restricted to those which he can prove for himself, the effect of education would be to impoverish and not enrich the mind; the educated man would be more ignorant than the man on the street who borrows his beliefs freely from others. But while education must invoke the authority of experts, it may initiate him into the secret of their expertness, so that he becomes the vicarious adherent of the experts' spirit of free inquiry.[58]

The task is to lead the student to appreciate that the authority of the experts lies in their adherence to the spirit of free inquiry. Within any field of specialized knowledge there is a community of expertise before which any claim to the advancement of knowledge in that field must be presented and defended. If every individual is not competent to judge on a matter then at least he may look to see that there are individuals judging the matter who are competent to do so. If he is to do this, then he must be given the chance to learn what it means to make such judgments. And, he is not going to learn to do this or to evaluate his stake in following the judgments of others if he is not given an opportunity to make such judgments at whatever level of competence he may have reached and in whatever contexts may be most crucial for his own well-being and that of society.

In particular he must gain experience in dealing with so-called controversial questions if only because "all important questions are controversial, if by 'controversial' is meant that there are at least two sides that can conceivably be taken." [59] If education for democracy is supposed to assist the individual to learn to make up his own mind then it must insist that he deal with questions on which the answers are not all in. He must deal with questions which require him to make up *his* mind for himself and not as the mere extension of the minds of his teachers.

It might be objected that this is extremely dangerous during the impressionable period of youth. To this one might respond that if the development and health of democracy depends upon the ability of men to make up their own minds, then this above all else should be impressed upon youth. Moreover, "all thinking is dangerous, if by 'dangerous' is meant the possibility of arriving at opinions different from those which prevail in the community." [60] There is always the risk in free inquiry of discovering mistakes or errors in the inquiries of the past. There is always the risk that matters may be seen in a new light and that new positions may be advanced in opposition to the old, or as more defensible than the old. There is always the risk that the teacher will learn something from his students about his subject that he had not thought of himself.

The only thing that cannot be seriously questioned, it would seem, is allegiance to the procedures of free inquiry itself. For, this would imply an attempt to justify or to question the justification of free inquiry either by appeal to free inquiry itself or by appeal to the unquestioning acceptance of some article of faith. Perry's theory of education was intended to ensure universal acceptance of the obligation to promote the ability and propensity of all individuals to engage in free inquiry. It was a call for faith in the processes of free inquiry as the instruments for improving the lot of all mankind. It was a call for the dogmatism of anti-dogmatism. This apparent paradox bears closer examination.

1. RV, p. 411; Perry's quotes.
2. Ibid.
3. Ibid.
4. Ibid., pp. 412–13.
5. Ibid., p. 421.
6. Ibid., pp. 423–24.
7. Ibid.
8. Ibid., p. 423.
9. Ibid.
10. Ibid., p. 430; Perry's italics.
11. Ibid., p. 412; Perry's italics.
12. Ibid.
13. Ibid.
14. **Ibid., p. 432.**
15. Ibid.
16. Ibid., p. 433.
17. Ibid., p. 429; Perry's italics.

18. Ibid., p. 413.
19. Ibid., Perry's quotes.
20. Ibid., pp. 433–34; Perry's italics.
21. Ibid.
22. Ibid., p. 434.
23. Ibid., p. 415; Perry's quotes.
24. Ibid.
25. Ibid.
26. Ibid., pp. 415–16; Perry's italics.
27. Ibid., p. 432.
28. Ibid., p. 416.
29. Ibid.
30. Ibid.
31. Ibid., p. 417.
32. Ibid.
33. Ibid.
34. Ibid.
35. Ibid., p. 416.
36. Ibid., p. 417.
37. Ibid., p. 432.
38. Ibid., p. 431.
39. Ibid., Perry's quotes.
40. Ibid., p. 430; Perry's italics.
41. Ibid., p. 431.
42. Ibid., pp. 430–31; Perry's italics.
43. Ibid., p. 426.
44. Ibid.
45. Ibid., p. 427, Perry's italics.
46. Ibid.
47. Ibid., p. 428.
48. Ibid., p. 427.
49. Perry, *One World in the Making*, p. 233.
50. RV, p. 414.

51. Ibid., p. 418; Perry's italics removed.
52. Ibid., p. 419; Perry's italics.
53. Ibid., p. 420.
54. Ibid.
55. Ibid.
56. Ibid., pp. 420–21; Perry's quotes and parentheses.
57. Ibid., p. 421.
58. Ibid., p. 428.
59. Perry, *The Citizen Decides,* pp. 108–9; Perry's quotes.
60. Ibid., p. 108; Perry's quotes.

VI. Perry and Education for Democracy

Fundamental critique of Perry's theory of education must refer back through it to his theory of value and theory of society. It must concern itself with the justification for his positions on education. And, the key problem in these theories lay in the tension between benevolence and prudence in the concept of harmonious integration.

The difficulties attending Perry's endeavors to deal with this problem have been indicated at length throughout the discussions thus far and it is scarcely necessary to reproduce the pertinent sections here. Instead, the problem will be restated and an attempt will be made to offer its solution. But before restating the problem it may be helpful to reintroduce it in a new light. The introduction begins with the following quotation from S. I. Benn and R. S. Peters:

> Philosophy, like science, is a clear example of rational discussion, and is conducted in accordance with the norms of impartiality and respect for truth. Philosophers flourish only in societies where the rational tradition has

taken root. And though, as philosophers, they are not committed to any particular maxims like 'debts ought always to be paid,' they are, as philosophers, committed to the very abstract procedural criteria implied in being reasonable. We have, however, been careful to stress the point that there is a gap between the bare impartial consideration of people as sources of arguments, which is strictly implied by being reasonable, and the richer impartial consideration of people as sources of claims and interests, the procedures implicit in being moral. Being moral is a species under the genus of being reasonable; it is not a synonym for being reasonable.[1]

Now, what sense can be made out of this subsuming of morality under the genus of being reasonable? Is morality *like* being reasonable in certain respects or is it a way of being reasonable in certain contexts? Is one to justify being reasonable by the principles of being reasonable and morality by the principles of being moral? Why cannot morality be justified by the principles of being reasonable?

The importance of ensuring morality was pointed up by these same authors in the following statement:

> Where large homogeneous interests conflict with smaller ones, democracy is always in danger of becoming mere majority rule. It can be preserved only if there are traditions of tolerance, and if the competing groups feel sufficient solidarity and concern about one another's welfare to be ready to compromise and respond to appeals to justice. This is another way of saying that democracy will work only if enough people want it to work, and are prepared to make the necessary adjustments that the claims of others demand.[2]

The basic problem for Perry may now be restated as follows: How is one to justify the attempt to insure that people will have the attitudes necessary to make democracy work and to justify the coercion or punishment of those who refuse to hold these attitudes at the same time as one insists on freedom of inquiry and the right of the individual to make up his own mind? This problem is in substance a summary of the problems of the paradoxes of freedom, tolerance and democracy as set down by Karl Popper.[3] His remarks on the paradox of tolerance are particularly instructive here, for they help to clarify the problem and although they do not provide the solution they do point the way:

> Unlimited tolerance must lead to the disappearance of tolerance. If we extend unlimited tolerance even to those who are intolerant, if we are not prepared to defend a tolerant society against the onslaught of the intolerant, then the tolerant will be destroyed, and tolerance with them. . . . [I]t may easily turn out that they [the intolerant] are not prepared to meet us on the level of rational argument, but begin by denouncing all argument; they may forbid their followers to listen to any thing so deceptive as rational argument, and teach them to answer arguments by the use of their fists or pistols. We should therefore claim, in the name of tolerance the right not to tolerate the intolerant [and to] . . . demand a government . . . that tolerates all who are prepared to reciprocate. . . .[4]

One cannot assume that all conflicts of interest can be resolved by rational demonstration that one and not the other is worthy of pursuit. If one person likes jazz, another likes

Mozart, they have one phonograph between them, and each sticks to his own taste, then they have a genuine conflict of interest, in which it may make no sense at all to talk about either one's justifying his claim that the other's interest is unreasonable. Without such conflict of interest the word 'compromise' would be meaningless. However, it is clear that by tolerating one another's interests through compromise each of them does get to hear what he wants to hear. This seems to be the 'reasonable' thing to do.

But now suppose a group of men committed to the canons of free inquiry. Suppose that their main concern is that the freedom of inquiry should flourish and be perpetuated. They sit down to determine what might be done optimally in behalf of these goals. If they take account of various possibilities, the odds would favor the attempt to make commitment to free inquiry as universal as possible so that their successes might at least outweigh their failures.

What form of government would they favor? Perhaps on a short run basis (especially in a society where they might comprise only a minute segment of the populace) they would prefer paternalistic rule by an oligarchy of those committed to these goals. But they are not committed to the perpetuation of such an oligarchy. Nor, are they necessarily committed to paternalistic rule by those who 'know better' for the sake of the well-being of the governed. Their own fundamental commitments require them to assist all people to 'know better.' To the extent that they are successful in their endeavors, the need for, or justification for, having such an oligarchy diminishes. As more people become committed to the canons of free inquiry the number of those qualified for membership in the ruling group increases. Among the matters into which they may inquire are those concerning their own well-being. Their ultimate choice of government would be some form of democracy, a government which encourages freedom of inquiry of all in the determination of the best interests of individuals taken together and severally.

Now a society of those committed to fostering and perpetuating allegiance to free inquiry cannot be a society of rational egoists. At the very least they must be concerned lest the activities of some of its members, or lest the consequences of environmental circumstances endanger the fundamental commitment of members. A starving man might quite readily follow the demagogue who promises to feed him; a poor man might wonder about the merits of such allegiance if his poverty does not permit him to get a fair hearing in a court of law or if he cannot afford to have his children avail themselves of the opportunities for education. The implanting of interest in the interests of others is a crucial requirement for the maintenance of a democracy based upon the goal of fostering and perpetuating commitment to the canons of free inquiry. *How* benevolent this interest must be will be considered more closely in a moment. There is another matter to be dealt with first.

The question might be raised as to why the fostering and perpetuation of commitment to free inquiry should be taken as a basic premise. In response one is tempted to ask, 'By what premises can it be established that it is not worthy of being fostered and perpetuated?' Clearly, *it* is not a denial of freedom except the questionable 'right' to be enslaved by ignorance or dogmatism. That the premise taken should be taken as a basic premise can only be denied by the assertion of the priority of some other premise. There is no obligation to accept this premise. One cannot argue that the premise justifies itself; this would be merely to reassert the premise while begging the question of its justification. One cannot justify his first principles by appeal to additional principles; if first principles had always to be justified there could be no first principles. There are two dangers in the failure to keep sight of this last point: sooner or later the argument degenerates into an infinite regression or else it turns back on itself in a circle.

As has been pointed out, Perry's philosophy suffered from both of these difficulties in its various aspects. Although he started out to develop a theory of value grounded in the natural interests of man it turned out that value was to be defined in its most important senses by man's attempt to control his natural interests. The definition of good became confused in an infinite regression of positive interest in positive interest in positive interest. His concept of moral obligation became confused in what was, in effect, an assertion that one ought to be benevolent and committed to the canons of free inquiry, because if he were benevolent and if he were so committed he would recognize his obligation to be benevolent and so committed.

The argument for democracy which has been proposed here is fairly compatible with Perry's philosophy. It is if anything an encapsulation of Perry's philosophy shorn of the fallacies inherent in the attempt always to prove first principles. It asserts the goal of fostering and perpetuating commitment to free inquiry. It recognizes the fact that individuals have interests. It indicates the need for interest in the interest of others. It leads to the conception of democracy as harmonious integration of interests in operation. It does permit the development of a conception of morality from commitment to free inquiry. It does *not* permit the demonstration of the necessity for commitment to free inquiry from that view of morality at the very same time. After all, an argument for justification must *start* somewhere.

One might want to question whether it does actually lead to the conception of democracy as harmonious integration of interests as Perry conceived it. This raises the problem of the interpretation of benevolence. Is one to have an interest in the other fellow's interest as the other fellow sees it or as the other fellow ought to see it if he only were more reasonable? Is there not a grave danger in even well meaning or benevolent Utopianism?

There is always the practical danger that those committed to the advancement of rationality and to paternalism toward that end might lose sight of the goal. There is always the danger that men of ultimate good will might adopt procedures in the short run that are inconsistent with the standards of that morality toward which they would progress. In sum there is the practical danger that those who act in the name of the interests of all the people might run roughshod over the interests of all the people. Still, what may be dangerous in practice is not certain to occur. So long as it is borne in mind that the primary goal is the spread of enlightment of all and not the fruits of the enlightenment of the few and that this entails the spread of enlightened self interest tempered by benevolent interest, then the obligation to seek to avoid these dangers is clear.

If we accept the task, how then shall we proceed? Cautiously, at least and at best. Ours is not a society of mindless and interestless individuals coming together for the first time to create the ideal polity. Diverse, indeed conflicting, interests and ideas abound. Different people have all sorts of stakes in the institutions and the structure of the institutions as they exist. But, some are greatly advantaged thereby and others are greatly disadvantaged.

In these circumstances the potential for social warfare is obvious. The advantaged are likely to feel secured in their advantages by a sense of institutional legitimacy. All too easily encroachments on these advantages are taken as illegitimate.

There may be a denial of the legitimacy of the interests of those who would encroach upon the privileges of the advantaged. At the extreme they may even deny the right of the disadvantaged to have interests that deserve consideration. The disadvantaged, on the other hand, may all too easily deny any obligation to consider the interests of those whom they would categorize as their oppressors. So long as the institutions of society do seem to work to the advantage of the haves, have-nots may commit themselves to the overthrow of these institutions. Each camp may be intolerant of the interests of the other, but worse than that the issue between them may turn into warfare in which the very survival of the structure of the society is at stake.

We tell ourselves that ours is, or at least is supposed to be, a democratic society. Our institutions are not supposed to work unfairly to the advantage of some and the disadvantage of others. In our commitment to the dissemination of democratic ideals we excite the expectations of the have-nots that their interests will be considered. We extol the right of free speech, thus providing opportunities for the have-nots to make their interests known. But the very same right permits them to give voice to their frustrations as the record of democratic accomplishment falls short of the democratic promise. And then if they grow weary of the pious promise and speak out against the ideology of tolerance, we invoke the right to suppress that intolerance in the name of that very ideology of democracy and tolerance.

But, do we have such a right? If in fact our sacred institutions are used as supports for our own intolerance of the rights of others to the consideration of their human interests, have we not denied ourselves the right to speak in the name of tolerance? These are not legal questions so much as they are moral questions. Any society can take steps to try to protect itself from those who would destroy it. It may, in fact, be impossible to have reasoned debate with those committed ideologically to the overthrow of democracy. Still, among those of us who profess our faith in the democratic ideals we can ask whether our professions of faith are made in good faith. Do we believe in these ideals or do we only believe in government of some of the people, by some of the people, for some of the people?

Here, then, is the moral dimension of democracy that Perry would force us to face. Democracy could not be a government of, by and for a part of the people. All must be included. The interests of all must be considered by all and for all, at least in effect through the representatives who were to represent the interests of all. He wanted a society of benevolent democrats. But, why did he insist on benevolence? Is a democracy of mutual tolerance not enough?

Perry wanted democracy to stand alone as that form of government and society which could lead to the development of the highest good of man and for man. He defined the highest good in terms of the satisfaction of the greatest number of the best interests of men. He wanted men committed not merely to the consideration of the interests of others, but as well to the goal of their satisfaction for the production of the greatest good. This is why he sought to distinguish 'freedom from' and 'freedom to' and why he emphasized the latter.

Despite the difficulties already demonstrated in maintaining a clear logical distinction between these 'two sorts of freedoms,' the import of Perry's attempt and its relevance to the contemporary scene strikes home. Again we remark that our society is a going concern. And, many are disadvantaged with respect to others. To tolerate another's interests may be merely to let him advance them if and as he can. If his history and heritage have left him and his children impoverished physically and intellectually, he may be free from legal restraint, yet surely he is not so free as a good many others to advance the well-being of his family as he conceives it. Nor, is he free to conceive that well-being as he might if his circumstances were better. As we work to eliminate the barriers of prejudice to the advancement of minority group members, we must remember that open housing laws do not of themselves make it possible for the poor to own houses and the accessibility of a library does not do very much for the poor illiterate.

The task of education in and for a democratic society was not merely to insure allegiance to the ideals of democracy. It was to fit each man to contribute to the society of greatest good. It required both the inculcation of benevolence and the development of the fullest possible intellectual potential of each future citizen. It required the development of each individual's potential to have interests to be pursued and considered in the best possible harmonization of interests of all. It demanded the development of reason and knowledge over rote and the presumption of knowledge. It denied the right of the agents of society to fit individuals into appropriate niches. It was to fit each individual to choose his niche in society subject only to the constraints of interest, innate potential, and benevolence. It was to free each individual to be a democratic citizen of a democratic society.

Underlying Perry's faith in democracy and his faith in education for democracy there is a still more fundamental faith, a faith in man. But, as Perry pointed out, it was not a blind faith:

> The power of man to shape his cosmic destiny is pitifully small, but in principle it is unlimited. For in proportion as man knows what the limits are, and what are their causes the way is open to remove them, by indirection, by organization, and by playing one natural

force against another. Man can now move mountains, having found the necessary lever and fulcrum. It is not impossible that he should someday learn to abolish death itself. It does not follow that he will do so, or is likely to do so. The issue remains in doubt, and man's personal choices, together with man himself, *may* go down to defeat and to final extinction. An empirical and naturalistic philosophy justifies no more than an attitude of disciplined hopefulness.[5]

In his realism Perry rejected the dogmatisms of false certainty. He himself preached the dogma of democracy whereby the intelligence and good will of men might be brought to bear upon the problems of creating the good life for all in the face of a necessarily uncertain future. He placed the destiny of man in the hands of men. If man is doomed by the forces of nature over which he has no control, then no dogma will save him. If man is to survive, then he must save himself by the intelligence and benevolence of his choices as he acts in the present with a view to the uncertain future. As educators our task is somehow to prepare men to accept the burden of responsibility for their future and somehow to fit them to carry it. We can not make their choices for them. We can guarantee neither the success of their future endeavors nor the success of our own educational endeavors. We can only try to make them as intellectually and emotionally capable as we can that they might have some chance of success. And then, we as educators will be entitled to no more than an attitude of disciplined hopefulness.

1. Stanley I. Benn and Richard S. Peters, *Social Principles and the Democratic State* (London: George Allen and Unwin, 1959), p. 56.

2. Ibid., p. 349.

3. Karl R. Popper, *The Open Society and Its Enemies* (Princeton, N.J.: Princeton University Press, 1950), pp. 545–47, chap. vii, n. 4.

4. Ibid., p. 546.

5. RV, p. 462; Perry's italics.

Index